The Rest of the Story

Bernard Tissier de Mallerais

THE REST
OF THE STORY

A Summary of the Life and Times of
Archbishop Marcel Lefebvre

Translated by Michael J. Miller

Angelus
Press

PO Box 217 | Saint Marys, KS 66536

Library of Congress Cataloging-in-Publication Data

Names: Tissier de Mallerais, Bernard, 1945- author. I Miller, Michael J.,
   translator.
Title: The rest of the story : a summary of the life and times of
   Archbishop Marcel Lefebvre / Bernard Tissier de Mallerais, Michael J.
   Miller.
Description: Saint Marys : Angelus Press, 2021. I Summary: "A short
   biography of Archbishop Marcel Lefebvre, founder of the Society of Saint
   Pius X"-- Provided by publisher.
Identifiers: LCCN 2021011318 I ISBN 9781949124774 (paperback)
Subjects: LCSH: Lefebvre, Marcel, 1905-1991. I Catholic
   Church--France--Bishops--Biography.
Classification: LCC BX4705.L474 T58 2021 I DDC 282.092 [B]--dc23
LC record available at https://lccn.loc.gov/2021011318

ANGELUS PRESS
PO BOX 217
SAINT MARYS, KANSAS 66536
PHONE (816) 753-3150
FAX (816) 753-3557
ORDER LINE 1-800-966-7337
www.angeluspress.org

ISBN 978-1-949124-77-4
FIRST PRINTING—April 2021

Printed in the United States of America

Contents

CHAPTER I

The Domestic Church

The vast plains of northern France, dotted with factory smokestacks whose exhaust fumes are swept into horizontal lines by the west wind, are constantly veiled in winter by a stubborn mist thickened with sooty clouds. However, this land, where Marcel Lefebvre was born on November 29, 1905, in the city of Tourcoing, between Lille and neighboring Belgium, is not gloomy. The windows, neatly aligned along endless red-brick façades, are decorated with joyful geraniums, and the well-kept, smart interiors assure families of a household life with plenty of cordiality and comfort, in which evening prayer brings each and every one together to smooth the day's difficulties and to pray above all for charity.

Baptism

In an unpretentious house on the rue Leverrier, Marcel was born on a somber November evening, too late to be baptized that same day. The next day, Louise brought the infant, reborn in Jesus Christ under the waters of Baptism, back to his mother.

"Madame," the servant girl said upon returning from Saint Christopher Church, "here is your little Marcel François Marie Joseph: a Christian now!"

"Yes, dear Louise. We named him 'Marcel' in memory of my visit to his church in Rome during my honeymoon: during the Roman persecution the poor Pope had been sentenced to tend pigs in the catacombs where he secretly celebrated the holy mysteries."

"And 'François'?"

"In honor of the Third Order of the Seraphic Patriarch of Assisi!"

"And 'Marie Joseph'?"

"So it is in all our families in Flanders: our children are entrusted to the Mother of God and to her virginal spouse!"

"Monsieur was not able to have his coffee this morning," Louise said, "He was already late for the factory."

"Yes," Gabrielle said, "our mill runs from six o'clock in the morning until evening; work is something that René has in his blood! For generations, in the Lefebvre family, and in my family, the Watines, we have spun and woven unceasingly, and in the case of my grandfather Lorthiois, the carpet factory was annexed to the house! Even our workers love their work and would be unhappy without work. I certainly hope that my little Marcel will not be a lazy boy!"

"No danger of that, Madame! 'The apple doesn't fall far from the tree.' He will be a tireless worker, I tell you: perpetual movement! Look at how he wriggles while waiting to feed!"

First Communion

Marcel grew up and studied with the Ursulines, nuns who had been laicized because of the anti-religious persecutions by the Masonic government of Émile Combes. Behind his imposing forehead covered with a neat fringe of hair, the boy was soon thinking about his First Holy Communion.

"You are very young, Marcel," seven-year-old Jeanne sententiously said, "to be approaching the Holy Table!"

"No, not at all! Soon I will be six."

"But you don't understand well enough what the Eucharist is."

"What I learned from Mama, in her catechism lessons, is that Jesus is in the Host, and that He wants to give Himself to my heart and me to His Heart. Do you know more about it?"

"Good," eight-year-old René interrupts, "but you will need special permission from the parish priest!"

And permission arrived: Pope Saint Pius X had just decided that young children who have reached the age of reason can receive Jesus in the Host.

"But you will have to go to Confession," René objected again.

"Mama has me make my examination of conscience."

And Marcel, seated at the table in the dining room, put his head between his hands, motionless.

"What is Marcel doing?" Bernadette, who was four years old, asked her big sister Jeanne.

"He is thinking about his sins, so that he can ask God to forgive them."

The next day, Father heard about Marcel's thievery in the pear orchards of his friend Jacques Dumortier, and how he was unwilling to put three-year-old Christiane's sheep near the crib of the Infant Jesus.

Through the grill of the confessional, Marcel saw the priest take his handkerchief and wipe his eyes: no doubt he was weeping over the sins of his penitent ... and Marcel made firm resolutions never to pull his sisters' hair and to abstain from the fruit of the trees in the orchards.

And on Christmas Day, December 25, 1911, Marcel had his first intimate conversation with the Eucharistic Jesus. What mystery took place between the child's soul and his Divine Savior? That afternoon, Marcel whispered to René: "What if I thanked the Pope?"

"You can't be serious!"

"Yes: for allowing me to receive Communion at the age of six!"

"Oh, well. Okay, let's write the letter!"

And René, who was going on nine, composed a letter to the Holy Father.

"Copy it, Marcel, and sign it yourself!"

And when it was done and duly signed "Marcel Lefebvre," René wrote the family's address on the back of the envelope addressed "To the Holy Father Pope Pius X, in Rome." The Italian post office would easily forward the letter! And some time later, in the house:

"Look," Gabrielle said to her husband, "a letter from Rome! And for Marcel!"

"What is this?"

"Do you know that before he was born, when I was carrying Marcel beneath my heart, I suddenly thought that, if it is a boy, he would be close to the Holy Father to help him in the Church?"

"Yes, you told me that, Gabrielle, but look: that has nothing to do now with our little Marcel. Come on! Open it!"

It was a letter from the Secretariat of State of Pius X, acknowledging receipt of the letter from the young first communicant and conveying to him the Apostolic Blessing of the Vicar of Christ.

Yes, Gabrielle thought, the Good Lord no doubt has plans for my Marcel.

CHAPTER II

Vocation
1914-1921

Marcel returns filled with excitement from Sacred Heart College.

"Mother, the Germans are occupying the whole college; our classes will be held in houses!"

The next day, at the corner of Reservoir Road, two soldiers with helmets seem to be waiting for him. He runs back home. That afternoon, Father Demarchelier comes asking after Marcel. "Why did you not come to school?"

"Because there were German soldiers in the road, and it was not yet six o'clock in the morning when the curfew lifts.... If they had caught me ..."

"Well, then! From now on take Abattoir Road."

Is that safer?

So each morning, Marcel overcomes the fear that grasps at him, and he goes to serve Mass at his favorite church at 6:30 a.m. each day.

The Trials of War

At age ten, he understands the tragedy of war. He does not eat his fill; people have "whole wheat bread," sticky beneath its black crust ... and some American chickens that arrive spoiled.

But all of a sudden Jeanne returns home:

"Here's the milk can filled from the 'soup kitchen'; we could use more, but so many people are lined up in the street!"

Supper ends quickly, the "big kids" do their homework silently at the same table by the dim light of a kerosene lamp.

"Now," says Madame Lefebvre, "time for prayer, children! Let us pray for your Uncle Louis; my poor brother is far away, over there, deported to the east, in Pomerania."

And the family kneels, arms outstretched, reciting the Rosary.

"Let's pray for Papa," says Bernadette. "Will he return from Holland?"

"Hush, my big girl! We must say nothing about it; your father is fighting for our country."

"Is it true that he's a spy?" Christine asks out of curiosity.

"Don't say that, my dear; it will only bring us trouble. René, are you the one telling your sisters these stories?"

"Mother, I know that Father, in his own way, is doing his duty for France!"

"That's good, children. I, too, do my duty as a nurse, in the 'Field Hospital' at the college. We should be sorry for those poor, wounded Germans."

"But Mother," Jeanne objects, "they are our enemies!"

"Did Jesus not tell us to love our enemies?"

Marcel says nothing, but he understands.

"You Have to Know How to Suffer"

Night falls, and the doorbell rings. It's a German officer.... He clicks his heels and salutes:

"Madame, I have a quartering order for you," he says in perfect French, "tomorrow you must take in four of our deaconesses."

With her blood boiling, Madame Lefebvre says nothing in reply. She guides her visitor to the third floor and shows him two empty, unfurnished rooms.

"Officer, sir, I have nothing else to give!"

And so, the next day, Marcel sadly witnesses as they come looking for Madame Lefebvre. They lock her in the basement of the town hall, where she will contract Pott's disease, a kind of tuberculosis of the spinal column. The doctor will order her to rest lying down for a year in a plaster corset.

"Yes," Marcel will say much later, "war is truly a terrible thing....
It left its mark on us, the five older children, and I think that my
vocation is due in part to it. Because we saw that human life is
insignificant, and you had to be able to suffer."

Almost Pope!

One day, as Marcel and Christiane study their lessons, each
at one end of the table, she asks him bluntly: "What do you think
you will do when you grow up?"

But immediately, she understands that he will not tell her
anything, he will only tease her. Because he is a terrible tease!
Nevertheless, with a sharp tongue she persists: "Do you think
you'll become a priest?"

"Oh, more than that!"

"But you want to be a bishop!"

"Well, Saint Paul says that a man can desire it."

"Then you want to be a bishop!"

"Oh, more than that!"

"There's no way that you can be Pope since only Italians are
popes!"

"Then *almost* Pope!"

Christiane, vexed, says no more.

Curiously, doesn't this reveal what he would be later on, without wanting it or even thinking about it, at the Holy Father's side?

Crusader of the Eucharist

Finally, the Armistice arrived, the end of the war, on November
11, 1918. Monsieur Lefebvre returned home; there were no end to
the joyful embraces.

At the college, the excellent Father Demarchelier would contribute further to revealing the adolescent's vocation. At the age
of thirteen, Marcel gladly became a "Crusader of the Eucharist."
He proudly wore the badge of the Crusade and ardently embraced
the Crusader's motto: "Pray, receive communion, sacrifice, be an

Apostle," which resonated with his one desire. Two years later, he was admitted to the "Saint Vincent de Paul Conference" at the college.

"Mother, would you like me to take care of the henhouse and hutch?"

"Why not? If you collect the eggs and feed the rabbits, I will give you some money."

"It's a deal," Marcel said. "And with that money, I will buy myself a bicycle."

"What will you do with a bike?"

"Visit the poor!"

On his day off, Marcel visited the neighborhood watchmaker, who had to close his stall; he was paralyzed, and his house was untidy.

"Let me do it, sir; I'm going to straighten it all up, but first I'll repaint your apartment!"

Soon his work for Robert Lepoutre was done. One day, Bernadette said to Marcel: "You don't know a watchmaker, do you? My watch is broken."

"Yes, I know one. Here's his address."

"I'll go right away."

Bernadette arrived at the street corner. There was no storefront, yet it was the correct address. She knocked. A voice called from within: "Come in." Bernadette pushed the door open to find a frail old man sitting in a wheelchair.

"Oh!" She cried out. "I must have made a mistake; I was looking for a watchmaker."

"But that's me! How can I be of service?"

"Here is my watch. It is broken."

"Give it to me, then come back in two days!"

The young woman returned.

"Here is your watch, Mademoiselle; it will work perfectly.... But, tell me, how did find my address? There is no longer a storefront here!"

"My brother gave it to me."

"Your brother? What is his name?"

"Marcel Lefebvre."

"Oh, you're Marcel Lefebvre's sister! Ah! Your brother is a saint! He came here one day, and seeing the place all dirty, he repainted everything; seeing that my fingers are still nimble, he found me some customers! I have a new life!"

Thus it is not through long speeches, but through charity in action that Marcel became an apostle to the poor. He did not boast about it at home: "Do not let your left hand know what your right is doing," Our Lord says.

Marcel was never happier than when he forgot himself so as to give everything to others. He was almost seventeen years old now. Would he become an apostle, a priest?

CHAPTER III

The Big Decision
1923

"This year, gentlemen, during the Easter vacation, you should make your decision concerning your future: Either you marry and carry on your family tradition, or else you follow God's call and go to work in the Lord's vineyard; your own vineyard in the religious life or that of others in the *priesthood!*"

Thus spoke Father Joseph Deconinck to his students in the graduating class. Marcel, touched, reported these comments back home. He was perplexed:

"A priest?" he said to himself: "That is so noble, how can anyone think of becoming a priest? No, I had better become a Benedictine!"

"If you have those doubts," young Christiane advised him, "go on a retreat at Wisques; Father guestmaster counsels the guests."

Marcel could have replied: "Little sister, mind your own business," but he was wise enough to apply the moral of La Fontaine's fable, *The Lion and the Rat*: "You often need someone smaller than you."

At the Abbey of Wisques

Marcel got on his bicycle and soon arrived at the great gate of the abbey, above which he read the inscription: "*Ora et labora,*" which he translated immediately: "Pray and work." They gave him a cell, and he attended the Divine Office of the monks and ate with them in the refectory in silence. He was struck by the atmosphere of peace and recollection. He read attentively the first chapters of the Rule of Saint Benedict concerning the novices: "If he truly seeks God..." At the end of three days, Father guestmaster came and knocked on his door:

"So, young man, does our life attract you? What appeals to you?"

Marcel answered frankly, "Yes, Father; I like very much your divine office chanted in two alternating choirs, in Latin, although I keep hitting wrong notes when I try to sing in unison from the nave!"

"We will teach you the psalmody!"

"Father, I love your ceremonies, your fraternal charity, everything.... But I would love to have an apostolate...."

"Ah! If that is the case, I fear that your place is not among us; we are cloistered, and our primary apostolate is prayer."

Marcel was disappointed. He went home.

"Well, what did Father guestmaster say?" his big sister Jeanne asked. (She was thinking of entering soon the Sisters of Mary Reparatrix in Tournai.)

"He said that I will not be a Benedictine."

"Not a religious, then?"

"Listen, sometimes I wonder whether I should become a simple brother with the Trappists. The brothers are so edifying, all united to God in their white and black habit and their work in the fields.... What if I went to Poperingue, to visit Uncle Alban and then to speak to Father Alphonse? They say he reads hearts."

With the Trappists?

He took his bicycle, crossed the Belgian border, arrived at the Trappist Monastery of Saint Sixtus, greeted his Uncle Alban, who was a lay brother there, and asked the brother porter: "Could I speak with Father Alphonse?"

"Yes, I will call him; have a seat."

Heavy steps were heard on the staircase. The good Father Alphonse had been a longtime missionary in the Belgian Congo, and he had returned to his homeland to become a Trappist. He

THE BIG DECISION 1923 **13**

opened the interior door of the parlor, looked Marcel in the eyes, and, before Marcel could ask the smallest question:

"You," he said, "you will be a priest. You must become a priest!"

This time there was no more hesitation. Marcel saw that he was confirmed in his true vocation, the one he had dreamed about throughout his youth. He had to talk to his father.

"You Will Go to Rome!"

"Papa, I will be a priest!"

"Good, Marcel! That does not surprise me. I thought that that might be for you."

"Well, then, Papa, I will enter the diocesan seminary, in Hellemmes!"

"No, no, no! You will go to Rome, where your brother René is staying!"

"But Papa, the studies at the Gregorian, in Latin, the very difficult examinations, what use would it all be? I would love to have a small parish, which I would take care of, somewhat like the Curé of Ars, and to try to become a saint, a holy priest, at least, in order to sanctify my parishioners: that is all!"

"Yes, but you are going to Rome, under the direction of Father Le Floch. You know very well that I fear the liberal orientation of the clergy in Lille. In Rome, you will work under the supervision of the Pope; you will learn sound Roman doctrine."

All that was left to do was for Marcel, accompanied by his father, to introduce himself to his bishop, Msgr. Quillet, who despite everything tried hard to maintain the diocese in its ancient fidelity to the Roman papal Magisterium.

"Yes, dear friend," the prelate decided, "go to Rome, feast on its rich food (*cf.* Isaias 25:6), become Roman!"

CHAPTER IV

Roman Seminarian
1923-1930

He made the train trip in the cheerful company of the two top scholars from the class at his college: Georges Leclerq and André Frys. As they approached Rome, they were at the windows trying to spot the dome of Saint Peter's.

"There it is!"

"Do you know," André asked, "that the French Seminary was founded and is directed by the Holy Ghost Fathers?"

"They are under the patronage of the Immaculate Heart of Mary, too," Marcel added. "It was first founded in 1703 on Pentecost by Claude Poullart des Places, who was not even a priest yet! But he wanted to form 'poor clerics,' penniless seminarians, 'in the principles of the soundest Roman doctrine.' That is what we need."

"And then," George remarked, "the son of the rabbi in Saverne, Father Libermann, who converted in 1826 and died on February 2, 1852, restored the missionary zeal of the Congregation and became its second founder."

"Yes," Marcel replied, "my brother René just entered their novitiate; he wants to go to Africa, to the blacks, the pagans! He will be a missionary."

A Militant Catholicism

At "Santa Chiara," the dignified, smiling Rector, Henri Le Floch, welcomed Marcel and the other "new men": "Get settled. But you will be two in each room. Our facilities are cramped, but not at all gloomy! We will all gather in the chapel each day for

15

prayer and the Holy Sacrifice. There is not much space in the choir stalls, either, but *Cor unum et anima una*: One heart and one soul, right?"

And once a week, the good, venerable Father Le Floch taught quite simply the Papal Encyclicals. At the end of three years, Marcel rejoiced.

"He is the one who taught us what the popes were in the Church and in the world; what the recent popes, in particular, have taught with remarkable continuity for a century and a half: anti-liberalism, anti-modernism! A militant Catholicism."

"Yes, the Father Superior makes us experience and enter into Church history, into the Church's battle for the Church and Christendom," said Raymond Dulac, one of the "older" students, "a battle against the perverse forces of the Revolution, which tries to overturn the Reign of Our Lord Jesus Christ."

"Listen," Marcel adds. "When I arrived, I was convinced that it was a very good idea for the State to be separate from the Church, that the State should be secular. Well, I was a liberal! ... These magnificent Encyclicals by Gregory XVI, Pius IX, Leo XIII, and Pius X, condemning those errors: *Mirari vos, Quanta cura* and the Syllabus, *Libertas*, finally the Letter about Sillon (the movement of Marc Sangnier) have opened my eyes. I am making my intellectual conversion!"

"Bravo, Marcel. For some could not stand the thought of waging this battle!"

"Yes, we had to choose: either leave the seminary if we did not agree, or else march, go into battle. I stayed. I think that my whole life will be oriented around this battle against this disastrous liberalism, which chants, 'Liberty, liberty for all!' But liberty is for the truth, the truth of Our Lord Jesus Christ and of His Church, not for error and false religions!"

"For me, too," Roger Johan remarked, "these Encyclicals were a total revelation. These popes taught us how to judge history, and as a result, what we learned will stay with us!"

"You see," Marcel concluded, "I feel that I am involved in a sort of crusade. I don't know when or in what circumstances I will have to fight, but I am 'on a crusade.'"

Jesus Christ the King

Father Voegtli, another professor at Santa Chiara, was very careful not to diminish the seminarians' enthusiasm. On the contrary, he increased it by speaking to them about Christ, Priest and King. In that year, 1925, he lectured to them, commenting on the Encyclical *Quas primas* by Pope Pius IX on the social kingship of Jesus Christ.

"His doctrine is simple," said Joseph Tailhades. "He speaks about nothing but Our Lord Jesus Christ the King. He shows us the role of the priesthood in this reign of Christ over souls and over society: 'The priesthood taken all the way, the integrity of the priesthood,' is 'the sacrifice of the priest for the reign of Our Lord Jesus Christ.' What a motto!"

"Yes," Marcel said, "what a tone of voice dear Father Voegtli speaks in when he tells us: 'My dear friends, I ask you to love Our Lord Jesus Christ, to preach His Name with all your hearts.' He also says: 'Our Lord must be the rule of our thought, the cause of our sanctity; nothing, nothing has ever been done without Him, who is the Word. Therefore all our thoughts, our meditation, our action must be for Our Lord Jesus Christ.' Well, that certainly transforms your life!"

"And Father Le Rohellec!" exclaims Victor Berto. "Like him, I am from Brittany, and a Thomist in theology, in other words, faithful to Saint Thomas Aquinas, the glory of the Dominican Order, who was teaching in Paris at the time of Saint Louis, King of France."

"It's also because of Father Le Rohellec," Marcel said, "that I discovered the *Summa theologiae* by Saint Thomas. 'Man is nothing without God, God is everything for him. Man is of God ... for God. Jesus Christ the Savior is, for man, for sinful man, the great means by which to return to his Creator and Lord.' What an admirable synthesis of all theology, of the science that is the understanding of faith! The 'all' of God in my life, the 'all' of Our Lord Jesus Christ in my salvation, in the salvation of souls! What a simple, profound, and true spirituality!"

"Do you know, Marcel," Father Berto insists, "that our fellow students call you 'the petrified Thomist'?"

"Petrified, oh no! Thomist, no! I simply like Saint Thomas; I stubbornly side with his teaching. Popes Leo XIII, Pius X, and now Pius XI call him the 'Common Doctor of the Church,' and they declare that 'Thomas, heir of the Fathers of the Church, by his synthesis of faith and sound human reason, has refuted all heresies in advance!' But more than that, I relish his aphorisms, his well-wrought sentences, his way of saying in a few words truths that have a marvelous depth! Read what he wrote about the Incarnation, the Redemption, and the little 'article' that he devotes to the Holy Sacrifice of the Mass: astounding!"

Priest for Eternity

Four years later Marcel Lefebvre was ordained a priest with four other men in Lille, on September 21, 1929, by his new Ordinary, Bishop Achille Liénart. The prelate chanted: "Grant to Thy servants, Almighty Father, and pour out upon them the dignity of the priesthood; renew in their hearts the spirit of holiness...."

Then it was done. Marcel was a priest for eternity.

Reluctantly, he left Rome, the "Eternal City" and with it, the relics of the martyrs and of the popes, the most eloquent voices of Tradition. It was difficult for him to go away—physically, not morally—from "this Chair of Peter and of this principal Church," as Saint Cyprian says, "from which the unity of the priesthood has its origin."

Would he be assigned immediately in his diocese?

After celebrating one of his first Masses at Jeanne's convent, in Tournai, he said another at the novitiate of the Holy Ghost Sisters, where Bernadette had entered.

She asked him: "Is it true that you are going back to Rome?"

"Yes, they advised me to pick up a doctorate in theology so as to serve the Church better. I will therefore be a seminarian-priest in Rome. What a grace!"

He passed his examination on July 2, 1930. Meanwhile he acted as "Master of Ceremonies" at Santa Chiara, under the senior direction of Father Joseph Haegy, who questioned Marcel after each ceremony that took place outside the seminary.

"Well, Father Lefebvre, how did His Eminence do?"

"The Cardinal was ill; Msgr. Pacelli replaced him. He did not 'do badly,' you can be sure, Father. But the schola was miserable: bad polyphony instead of our beautiful Gregorian chant! Why don't they follow the instructions of Pius X?"

"You do well to have convictions. It is necessary to combine liturgical piety with doctrine! I like young priests of your caliber: pious but unostentatious, with well-defined principles and firmly-founded convictions, and with it, peaceful calm in the midst of ecclesiastical uncertainties. May God protect you for His Church!"

"I will tell you a secret: my spiritual director, Father Liagre, is teaching me the love that God showed us in Our Lord Jesus Christ. 'God is charity,' "He loved me and gave Himself for me.' Now it is my turn to give myself! But pray for me; I do not know what awaits me in Lille; His Excellency is thinking about appointing me professor at the college.... I have neither the desire nor the qualifications to teach."

Thank God, Marcel received in late summer of 1930 his assignment as second assistant priest in a working-class parish in the suburb of Lille. To work!

CHAPTER V

A Momentous Corpus Christi
1931

Father Deschamps, first vicar of Our Lady of Lourdes at Marais de Lomme, protested frankly: "No, *Monsieur le Curé*, Father Marcel is right: let's re-establish the Corpus Christi Procession this year."

"But you do not know," responded the pastor, Father Delahaye, "that less than five years ago the Communists prevented us from leaving the church. Since then, the procession has been held in the church."

"*Monsieur le Curé*," interjected Father Lefebvre, "trust me; I have put together a muscular security squad of young men with yellow and white arm bands. They will be ready to come in against all aggression!"

"I want to avoid all bloodshed!"

"Everything will go peacefully, dear *Monsieur le Curé*. I had all the altar boys rehearse, especially the two thurifers who will take turns incensing the Most Blessed Sacrament, and the little girls know how to throw their flower petals towards the monstrance; and several families are already preparing the four altars of repose, not counting our Young Christian Workers who are coloring their sawdust to decorate the path for our dear Lord."

"I commend it all to the grace of God," the pastor finally said.

And all went well. Even one of the municipal brass bands of Lomme, made up of radicals, accompanied the hymns. The band of the Christian Democrats declined. The procession reached the third altar of repose, on the steps of the Château de l'Ermitage, and it was splendid. Then it set out for the one at the pub *L'Étoile*, when suddenly a shot was fired!

Startled, the pastor jumped to one side, and Jesus in the Host with him—so to speak.

"Oh, Father, I told you so!" he whispered to Marcel who, to his left, was serving as subdeacon: "the Communists!"

The security squad rushed toward the aggressor ... who proved to be an overly enthusiastic parishioner who had thrown a firecracker!

At the sacristy, the pastor, Father Delahaye, mopped his brow. "You really scared me, dear Father Lefebvre!"

"I had nothing to do with it, *Monsieur le Curé*; your troops are the ones to blame!"

"Hmm," the pastor murmured to Father Deschamps, "I think that behind his unalterable calm, our Father Marcel is very good at sending our people off to fight for the faith!"

The Call of Africa

But Marcel was to continue his militant experiments on distant shores.... Indeed, for a year his brother, a missionary in Gabon, had been writing him time and again, bombarding him with letters:

"What are you doing still in France? Here we are in the thick of the battle against the witch doctors and also in confrontation with Protestant pastors! And then our army of catechists prepares for us large numbers of catechumens, children and adults, for baptism. Join us!"

Marcel read and reread these appeals. To his mother, who asked him about it, he confided:

"I am completely happy at Marais, but in Africa I would have a more useful combat, a much more meritorious life. I could give myself more. It is the voice of God, I ought to follow it. Of course, it is painful for me to detach myself from my parishioners in Lomme. But let us make this sacrifice!"

Marcel wrote to Msgr. Achille Liénart, who had recently been created a cardinal. He received a reply on July 13, 1931:

"His Eminence has charged me to tell you that he authorizes you to leave the parish as of July 20 to enter the novitiate of the Holy Ghost Fathers."

CHAPTER VI

At the Seminary in Libreville
1932-1938

There he was: Marcel Lefebvre, a priest-novice, in Orly, near Paris. The airport did not exist yet, but only some "gyroplanes," the ancestors of helicopters, which whirred and went in circles around the park. One got used to it; but not to the icy winter and to reading Rodriguez (*Christian Perfection,* in four volumes) while walking single file in the courtyard of the novitiate, since the cape could scarcely protect his hands against chilblains.

Priest and Spiritan Novice

"It was through the torture of the cold that they are preparing us for the stifling heat of Africa!" Gérard de Milleville thought out loud.

"And at night," retorted Marcel, "I put four, five blankets on the bed; it's a huge weight, but it doesn't make me warm!"

"And with that, no heating! Is it possible to make novices suffer like this?"

"Bah," said Marcel, "it is an opportunity to live the three mottoes of Father Libermann, the founder of our order: 'renunciation, peace, union with God!'"

That was where he acquired, with the expansion of his soul, the principles of the spiritual life which he regretted not having received systematically in Rome. He was captivated by God's love for mankind, manifested by the Incarnation and the sorrowful Passion of God the Son, Jesus Christ. He meditated on and assimilated this passage by Saint John, from which he would later draw his episcopal motto: "God is charity. By this hath the charity of God appeared towards us, because God hath sent His only begotten Son into the world, that we may live by Him. . . . And we have known and have believed the charity which God hath to us. God is charity: and he that abideth in charity, abideth in God, and God in him" (I John 4: 8-16)."God is charity." Now the property of charity, the property of love is to give oneself. So the Spiritan Marcel Lefebvre, like the teenager formerly, would give himself to souls to attract them to Jesus Christ, to God.

"Ah, you wish to give yourself?" exclaimed the director of the house, Father Oster. "Perfect! Since you have a doctorate in philosophy and in theology, I appoint you professor of Sacred Scripture for your novice classmates!"

"Yes, Father," stammered Marcel, taken aback.

The archives still possess the little notebook with the close, regular handwriting of the spur-of-the-moment professor. But it made him ill! He had persistent migraines and had to take to his chaise longue in the afternoons. He was very humiliated by the mocking looks of his confreres. "Bah," he said, "this will pass when I get to Africa!"

"But really," he added, "I am not made for teaching!"

Finally, in September, he made his profession of the three vows of religion: poverty, chastity, and obedience. Now he was a priest and a religious. With emotion, he then pronounced his "consecration to the apostolate."

"Farewell then, my country, where I leave so many memories, childhood friends, beloved parents! Farewell. . . . For the love of God, I solemnly consecrate myself to the apostolate in the Congregation of the Holy Ghost and the Immaculate Heart of Mary and I make myself forever the servant of abandoned souls."

Professor and Mechanic

The Foucault steamboat, spewing from its three chimneys a sooty smoke, discharged its passengers at the port of Owendo, about three miles from Libreville.

On the quay, Bishop Tardy kept an eye out for his new missionary: Ah! There is a white soutane, with the Spiritan black sash; it's he! And he has a handsome brown beard!

"Welcome, Father Lefebvre! What a reinforcement you will be for our apostolic vicariate!"

"At your orders, Your Excellency!" Father Lefebvre had not forgotten the military obedience when he was in the armed services in 1926-1927.

"Good! I like that. Well, I tell you right now: Since you are a doctor of philosophy and theology, they tell me, I am appointing you professor in my seminary!"

"Ouch! Your Excellency! Oh, no!"

The Bishop smiled encouragingly: "I will show you the premises."

On the hillside the humble cathedral with its plank walls shone in its immaculate whiteness; somewhat behind it, the house of the Bishop and the Fathers; upstairs, projecting balconies provided coolness for the common rooms on the ground floor; and a four-sided roof, with a central ridge and projecting broadly, sheltered the whole building.

But the seminary was to the left, a little lower, made of light material for its entire height and length; that was where Marcel was going to toil, because Bishop Tardy said to him right away:

"With dear Father Fauret, who is here, you will teach all the courses of the minor and major seminary! From grammar to canon law, to geometry and physical sciences!"

By some miracle, Marcel did not flinch. Down to work!

He adapted to the heat, the humidity, the mosquitoes, which were more dangerous than the agile panthers or the crocodiles: they injected you with malaria and FBH or blackwater fever (a fatal complication of malaria), and the tsetse flies carried sleeping sickness. At the time, there was a great risk, not only of having to endure every evening the torture inflicted by those little creatures, but of dying a martyr from one of those infections, without the glory of having shed your blood for Christ!

"Too bad," the young professor said to himself, "the essential thing in God's sight is my work: to transmit as simply as possible what I received at the College and in Rome!"

Well, he proved to be an excellent teacher of future priests. The witnesses speak.

"So, Father Fauret, how is Father Lefebvre managing?"

"Ah, *Monseigneur*! It is a pleasure to work with him, we tease each other all the time."

"And your opinion?"

"He is a man who is very flexible, pleasant, smiling, measured, but firm in his ideas, well liked by his students, very personal in his evaluations and his decisions; and what is more, outstanding from the perspective of organization and material equipment. In no time at all, he repaired the recalcitrant engine of our old Citroën."

"Good! Well, Father Fauret, he will succeed you as rector of the seminary, and you will become my Vicar General!"

"Ah! Don't do this; I have no diploma, and I must confess to you, Your Excellency, that at the scholasticate (seminary), I skipped many courses in canon law.... Take Father Marcel instead!"

"I will not choose a stubborn coworker!"

Of course this was an excuse; the Bishop wanted Marcel to be rector of the seminary. But it is true that Marcel, with the natives, with his seminarians, was unshakable in his decisions: "Yes is yes, no is no." One day, the young seminarian Ange Mba burst out laughing upon seeing Father Marcel eat cassava—they had forgotten to buy bread.

"Well, Ange, what are you laughing at? You are making fun of the superior?"

"Ah yes, Father, I see how you are eating cassava!"

"Ange! I see that the seminary is not the right path for you!"

And on the spot, Ange ceased to be a seminarian. This would not prevent him from becoming one day the father of Casimir Oyé-Mba, the future Prime Minister of Gabon.

Some Sensible Advice

In 1938 Father Marcel preached to the deacons the retreat in preparation for their priestly ordination. The theme, original but essential, was this: "The charity of God, model and source of apostolic zeal"; and in contrast, "one of the wounds inflicted on our human nature by original sin which we call 'wound of ignorance' and its remedy, 'supernatural wisdom'"; then: "I belong to God, I am made for God; but poor sinner, I need humility and obedience; thus, God is all, man is nothing!"

His practical advice was contained in some very sensible principles, which he explained:

1. True zeal does not exist apart from obedience.
2. It is necessary above all to love the truth, and really to see it as the salvation of souls. Conscience saves no one, only the truth saves. And it is not true charity to keep souls in error or in sin.
3. It is necessary to see the faithful from the perspective of the state of grace: what we call "justification," the passage from the state of sin to the state of grace.
4. Let us not have personal principles but those of Our Lord and of the Church. This is true charity, and not the sort of charity preferred by liberals or modernists.
5. The Pope is the successor of Peter, Christ on earth, the immovable rock, the light of the world.
6. The Bishop is coming to visit your mission. Tell him about your work, ask his advice.

Following these recommendations, of which the fifth obviously lacks a further qualification that would prove necessary after the Second Vatican Council, Father Lefebvre would leave the seminary; he felt very tired.

"Your Excellency," he finally told Bishop Tardy, "I am exhausted by these six years at the seminary. Last night, I felt that I was dying, and I knocked on the wall to call Father Berger."

"It's true, Your Excellency, Father Marcel asked me for Extreme Unction; to calm him I gave him some herbal tea.... But a little vacation would do him some good."

"Vacation! You're not serious! Father Marcel, you have not yet spent the ten years in the vicariate required by statute. You will stay in Gabon! But," he added obligingly, with a smile in his eyes, "if you are exhausted, go and rest ... in the bush!"

CHAPTER VII

On the Banks of the Ogooué
1938-1945

Father Francis Ndong, ordained a priest in June, welcomes his new Superior—who was his Rector at the Seminary!—as he makes landfall from the Ogooué to the lovely Mission House of Saint Michel de Ndjolé.

"Welcome, Father Lefebvre. Look at the beautiful brick church built by your predecessor, Father Petitprez, who worked himself to death."

"Oof! Then I must follow suit.... Well then, with God's grace!"

"Rest assured, my good Father, that everything is running well here; I am responsible for the boys' boarding school while the Sisters tend to the girls' school. And you, Father, you have the rounds to make and the Mission. You see, we Africans are not made for that work. Leave the Mission to the Europeans!"

"You're very frank, my dear Father, but I don't dislike that: that is why I have come here! To enlarge the reign of Christ!"

In a Canoe to Save a Dying Man

No sooner did he finish speaking than someone else appears at the dock.

"Father, come quickly! Old Albert Obamba is dying! Far from here, in Bôoué."

"Bôoué, dear Lord, that must take at least five hours by canoe."

"Antoine N'konkou will accompany you," Father N'Dong says, "with the chapel case and the sacred oils."

They start the journey and must travel upstream and cross the rapids by portaging the canoe. In Bôoué, a man waits at the pier. Father Marcel calls out to him:

"Where is old Albert Obamba, who is dying?"

"That's me, Father," the supposedly-dying man replies, "I wanted to talk to you!"

And Father Marcel, faced with such thoughtless simplicity but master of himself, finds only these words in reply: "Albert, this is not an emergency!"

Normally, however, the missionary's visits to the villages are announced in advance by tom-tom. From one village to the next, along the rivers and hilltop paths, the happy news of the missionary's journey resounds in a drumbeat. The priest quickly settles into the hut for distinguished guests, but must swiftly evacuate in the middle of the night to flee an invasion of fire ants! The next day, in the "chapel hut" (with walls made of straw and a roof of banana leaves), the priest recites his breviary, prays, prepares for Mass, then sits beneath a palm tree, behind an improvised grille, for an endless session of sacramental confessions. Towards the end, the penitents who arrive are men; it is sometimes "faster."

"Father," says the twentieth, "as for me, it's the same thing" (implying: as the previous penitent)!

Then Holy Mass is celebrated, the "Sacrament of the Passion of Christ," as Saint Thomas says, the sacramental sacrifice which makes present the Priest and Victim of the Cross, Jesus Christ, and which re-presents, by the outward symbols of the separate species of bread and wine, signs of His death, His bloody sacrifice on the cross, and which applies the merits thereof, as taught by the Council of Trent in 1562 and Pope Pius XII in 1947.

The altar boys, duly trained by the village's master of ceremonies, respond to the priest who begins by saying:

"Introibo ad altare Dei."

"Ad Deum qui laetificat juventutem meam."

Yes, the altar of the Divine Sacrifice of the Bread of Angels which will nourish them gives joy to the youth of the acolytes.

Discernment

Who knows: maybe one of them, who is the star student at the village school, might hear Father call to him:

"Félicien, my lad, take me to your parents' home!"

And in the family hut (four wooden stakes, straw walls and a roof made from used corrugated iron that leaks in places when it rains) the missionary sits and speaks with them:

"For the Saint Michel Mission House, you come to Ndjolé to the 'village of the Christians' (that is rebuilt each year)! And I keep your son Félicien in the secondary school of the mission, over there; afterwards, we will see!" He says all this in the "Fang" language, which he speaks like a native.

That is how Father Lefebvre prepares the young people who tomorrow will be the leaders in Gabon. And on the feast of Saints Peter and Paul, when parents come to take their children back home for the vacation:

"You, Théodose, are leaving school. You must have a trade, so you will remain at the mission workshop as an apprentice. And later, you are still poor? Hah, but not a lazybones: so as to work and get married."

"Yes, Father!"

And a few years later, on the feast of Saints Peter and Paul:

"You, Félicien, go to Libreville, to the seminary!"

"Yes, Father!" the boy replies with a big smile.

Father Lefebvre can tell; he sees the boys who have the necessary dispositions: piety, studiousness, honesty, purity. And it is similar for the girls:

"You, Ernestine, will enter the novitiate of the Sisters of Saint Mary of Gabon!"

"Yes, Father!"

This is how a Christian society is built: by the eye, the tact, and the decisions of the missionaries. And, as Father Marcel says, thanks to two essential instruments: the catechists and the schools:

"First, thanks to our seventy catechists, divided into five regions under the direction of five head catechists, such as the dear Thomas Atondo-Dyano who oversees the Petite-Rivière and Onanghé Lake!"

And, he adds, thanks to our schools:

"They are the major path for the complete Christianization of the country. Without them, we could not hope to preserve the great influence that Catholic Missions currently have. It is extremely important for the Church."

"He Brings Us Light"

Father Marcel would be successively named Superior at Donguila, then at Saint Mary in Libreville, and finally at Saint Francis Xavier in Lambaréné, not far from the hospital of Dr. Schweitzer, a Protestant pastor and physician who cares for lepers. Father Marcel would greet him: "Pastor, I understand that you play the organ, and very well at that."

"Oh, I am not a professional organist!"

"That doesn't matter; would you agree to come play our humble harmonium at the church during the holidays?"

That was the incipient ecumenism of Marcel Lefebvre!

And the Pastor comes during the holidays to play the harmonium at Saint Francis Xavier: and in this sense, it's permitted! But be careful, for Father Lefebvre has written a pamphlet titled *"Ollé Lang"*: "Everyone can read it," in which he explains that "Luther stole the Bible and went off to make his own church." Also on the river, when a canoe of Catholics comes across a canoe of Protestants, the Catholics cry:

"Heretics! Heretics!"

"That may not be charitable," says Father Marcel, "but at least ours know they are Catholics!"

So after Ndjolé, Father Lefebvre is assigned to Donguila, on the banks of the Como Estuary, which tends to silt up. One day, while crossing from his motor boat to the pier at Donguila for

Confirmation, Bishop Tardy and his beautiful purple cassock—horrible—fell into the mud!

"Never mind," decided Marcel, "we're building a wharf!"

One month later, there he is, next to an improvised cement mixer, waist-deep in the mud and supporting a cement drum on top of the two earlier ones:

"Come on, pour! Fill this last drum with concrete for me! Then we'll set on it and the one opposite it the twentieth beam, then we'll cover the twentieth span of our pier with boards. That will be solid and durable!"

Six years later, in Lambaréné, he is appointed official Superior of the Mission. Two months after that, he remarks:

"Will we continue to use only oil lamps for light?"

"Do you have some other idea in mind, Father?" says Brother Norbert, who knows how to do everything: fell trees, saw tree trunks, construction of all sorts.

"Yes, my brother; for our wood shop and our boat factory, you need more electricity! And in other places, too. . . ."

And as he did in Libreville, he arranges for his brother Michel, an industrialist in Northern France, to send a very simple but large "electric generator" that runs on gas. Then he teaches a course on electricity and on Catholic scientists. Then he turns on the system at night and illuminates not only the whole Mission but also the town!

"Ah," the natives exclaim, "that's the man from Lambaréné, he brings us light!"

A Letter from France

But one day in 1945, as he returns from a tour of the villages on Lake Onangué, on the Wombolié—the river of hippopotamuses, which can capsize your boat by ramming it with their spines—Marcel saw a nimble canoe approaching his motor boat.

"What is the matter? What has happened?" he asks.

"A message for you, Father," says a native standing in the canoe that he propels like a gondola with a pole.

Marcel looks at it: "A letter from France, from Paris."

He opens it, and the thin sheet of paper nearly slips through his hands; it's from Bishop Le Hunsec. He deciphers the Superior General's hurriedly written script: "You have been appointed Superior of our Scholasticate of Philosophy in Mortain. Return swiftly!"

"Scholasticate! Mortain! But what about Africa?" the missionary groans.

"What's the matter?" asks Pierre-Paul, his "sacristan," the jack-of-all-trades who accompanies him.

"Damn it! I'm starting to cry," mutters Marcel; "this can't be!"

Moved to tears by having to leave the Africa where he'd like to die, Marcel makes his sacrifice then and there. "It's nothing," he answers, "I'm being recalled to France."

At the Mission, his confreres express their condolences, but he stops them: "Listen, I have resolved never to ask why my superiors assign me to a new post, and wherever that may be, to go to work, without fretting, without regretting too much the post that I must leave. Besides, with God's grace! Everyone lives with his own temperament, his character, according to his formation, and God grants the grace of his state of life that he needs to accomplish the task. Throughout all this," he said, "a man works under the watch of God, not to complete a career but to save souls!"

CHAPTER VIII

His Battle of Mortain
1945-1947

On a beautiful late late-autumn day, November 11, 1945, Father Émile Laurent and his companion traveled the Norman countryside by automobile. The early morning mist rose to reveal verdant meadows, flowering bushes, sunken roads, mud-walled houses with thatched roofs, and cattle that tirelessly graze on the grass and transform it into creamy milk, truly a miracle of biology! But alas, here and there were towns in ruins, devastated farms, and the abandoned carcasses of armored vehicles.

"Finally, my dear Fr. Lefebvre," said the Provincial Father of France, "you will see our house: the Abbaye Blanche, spared by last year's bombardments—a miracle of Our Lady of La Blanche. To tell the truth, there is not one pane of glass left in the windows. But, you are just the man for the occasion. I'm counting on you."

"You have dealt me a bad hand," replied Marcel, "but I will make sure to feed my hundred hungry young men, these seminarians who are back from the war! I will find them blankets for their beds, the brothers will make a lot of partitions and cupboards for them, and I'll find some basins and jugs so that they can wash in the morning!"

The carriage passed through the gaping portal (its double doors were off their hinges) and stopped at the foot of the tall, dark façade of the "Scholasticate of Philosophy" in Mortain. Introductions and handshakes followed. And now to work!

"It is difficult to get supplies, Father Lefebvre," said the financial director Father François. "The city is in ruins...."

"I was thinking about that. Have you received the van that I requested from my brother? It is my father's automobile, which Michel, my brother, had converted and fitted with a wood-gas generator."

"We Can Tell That He Loves Us!"

And every morning, after his Mass, the Father Superior, at the wheel of this hybrid vehicle, made the circuit of the surrounding farms, collecting bread, flour, eggs, chicken, milk, Camembert cheese, vegetables, and fruit. He had a refrigerated area installed for the meat.

"He is really feeding us," exclaimed André Buttet; "Now *that's* an organizer! We may be cold this winter, but we are not hungry!"

"Yes," Emmanuel Barras, a Swiss seminarian, added, "he is 'super.' And when you hear how the Superior spends his time rushing through the countryside in the car that belonged to his father who was deported and then martyred, it energizes you. And then he rolls up his sleeves! He's 'tip top'!"

"And that ten-day pilgrimage to Mont Saint-Michel," said Maurice Fourmond, "with provisions brought up by bicycle—he planned it for us and made it happen!"

"He cares about us, you can really tell that he loves us!"

Thanks to this devotion, Father Lefebvre managed to communicate with those young minds whom the crisis of authority in France during the war had made a bit refractory.

General de Gaulle's success did not erase the memories of old Marshall Pétain's stoic resistance. The remnants of the mutual hostility of the young men must be overcome "from the top." Marcel was very good at it: during the first spiritual conference of the evening, they heard Fr. Lefebvre begin his remarks in a very personal way that appealed to them:

"I'm an African bushman trying to rebuild his life in France."

And he continued on a supernatural note:

"You owe every minute of your life to the souls that are waiting for you. . . . As for me, whatever I have to give, I give freely!"

Father Marcel and Politics

Having thus won over his audience of "old" combatants or of young recruits, he could take their questions and first help them understand the Church's sound social doctrine, which had been distorted by Communist propaganda.

"Some within the Church now claim that it is enough to baptize Communism and that doing so will bring about a 'New Christianity'! You know well that Pope Pius XI condemned this utopian idea and stated clearly that 'Communism is intrinsically wrong'!"

"But Father, you're talking politics!"

"And what of it? You can understand this: if 'politics' means republic or monarchy, one form of government or another, or at worst, party politicking, then priests do not get mixed up with that. But if 'politics' means a Catholic state or an irreligious (and therefore atheistic) state, then, in that case, it's macro-politics; a priest must not remain silent, he must preach Christ the King!"

Most of the young men recognized that Father Lefebvre was clarifying their ideas.

"We greatly appreciated him," reported one of the older seminarians, "we truly liked him because he was very simple and very direct."

"He presented authority to us in a sympathetic light," added another witness: "we lived then in a France torn apart by a crisis of obedience caused by 'Free France.' In order to restore the sense of obedience, he had to show us the true face of authority. He set an example and we understood that language. I remember an 'assignment' that he gave us one day in class: 'Give me your comments on this definition of authority:

"'We can say about authority that it is entirely divine in its principle, powerful and smooth in its essence, admirably productive, and a herald of order, prosperity, and peace if it is guided by the gift of counsel and is supported by prudence.'"

"This definition that he gave us was quite unexpected, but isn't it superb?"

The Will of the Pope

In Mortain, Father Marcel Lefebvre was able to combine seemingly contradictory dispositions in an uncommon harmony: doctrinal firmness with kindly charity that lubricates the gears; practical adherence to demanding principles with a most caring paternal love.

Then, on June 25, 1947, a simple telephone call bursts in like a thunderclap.

"Hello, Father Lefebvre? This is Bishop Le Hunsec, your Superior-General. Are you sitting down, Father? I have some news. The Pope has appointed you...."

"What? ..."

"Yes, appointed you the Vicar Apostolic of Dakar, in other words, a Bishop."

"Oof, oof!"

"It's the will of Pope Pius XII, and you are a religious, so you must obey!"

And that evening in the refectory, a bell rang at the professors' table. Father Macher rose and, his voice trembling with emotion, announced the news to the community. Father Lefebvre then rose in turn.

"I cannot refuse my duty.... But I remember the words of the Gospel: 'And they led him out to crucify him.'"

In conclusion, he said the same thing that he had said on arriving in Mortain:

"Whatever I have to give, I give freely!"

CHAPTER IX

Vicar Apostolic, Then Archbishop of Dakar 1947-1962

On December 18, 1947, Cardinal Achille Liénart, the Bishop of Lille, was still quite Catholic but with a few nuances.... He would consecrate Marcel Lefebvre a bishop in the Church of Notre Dame des Anges in Tourcoing.

The Cardinal asked, "Will you take the *Oath Against Modernism?* It is required. Place your hand upon the Bible!"

"Gladly," Marcel replied.

"I firmly hold, then, and shall hold to my dying breath the belief of the Fathers in the charism of truth, which certainly is, was, and always will be in the succession of the episcopacy from the apostles. The purpose of this is, then, not that dogma may be tailored according to what seems better and more suited to the culture of each age; rather, that the absolute and immutable truth preached by the apostles from the beginning may never be believed to be different, may never be understood in any other way."

"No doubt.... But we have to be able to adapt this truth to the modern world," said Cardinal Liénart, frightened by the absoluteness of this truth.

"Our task, Eminence, is to adapt the ages to the Word of God, as Saint Paul says (Heb. 11:3); isn't that my mission among the Muslims and pagans of Senegal?"

The "Front Lines" of the Missions

One year later, Bishop Lefebvre had hardly finished visiting the missions and priests of his Apostolic Vicariate, whether on the "Little Coast" along the Atlantic or in the sands of Thiès and Kaolack, when the young priest Henri Gravrand arrived in Dakar, fresh from his novitiate and his studies.

"Your Excellency," he said, "I have just arrived. I'm telling you right away: I want to go to the front lines of the missions, yes! The work of converting all these people!"

The Vicar Apostolic took care not to chill the young missionary's zeal, which he shared: we need priests of this caliber, or else we accomplish nothing!

"Good!" he replied, "then you shall go to the pagans. I will take you to a place that has not launched well."

So the two went to Diohine, to the southeast; the bishop was at the wheel of the Vicariate's Jeep.

"This is a lovely mission," he said as they arrived, "but you will not be alone for long, your superior, Father Schouwey, will return shortly from his leave."

One week later, the bishop returned to check on everything. "How is it going?"

"Ah, Your Excellency! Let me tell you: your mission looks like a routed army."

The bishop was somewhat taken aback, but he liked this frankness and he was not a man to clip the wings of a young coworker:

"Well then, it is up to you to rally them! Start something at Fatick on the banks of the Sine. The pagan king Makekor Diouf had told Father Schouwey: 'Even on your side of the river, you are not to build anything that an arrow could not pass through!' Only huts are allowed. And crossing to the other bank is out of the question! But ultimately, it's up to you!"

The Miracle of the King of the Sine

One fine day in 1949, encouraged by the implicit support of his bishop, Father Gravrand decided to cross the bridge.

"I'm crossing my Rubicon, like Caesar," he said to his guide; "but this time, it's being done in a carriage!"

There the two sat in their carriage, which balanced on its two big wheels, drawn by their Rocinante. The air was fresh that day, just the right atmosphere for a conquest. The priest improvised a victory song with an accented note on the word "king": "I am the King of the Sine!"

His companion interrupted him. "Father, the King of the Sine is standing in front of you!"

Indeed, walking directly towards them was a grizzled old man, the King of the Sine in person.

In a flash, the missionary turned the threat into a Providential opportunity: he jumped down from the carriage.

"Sire," he said, bowing, "I've been looking for you."

That was not entirely true, and so he added, frankly: "I'm going off to start recruiting for the Christian Church."

And for a second the king vacillated: "Very good," he said. "What is your name?" he asked the missionary's young companion.

"Jean Soundiata Keita."

"Ah!" said the king. And he thought: this boy is from the royal line of the founder of the great dynasty in the thirteenth century!

Then he gave his orders to the young man:

"Go see the Bour (the king) of Pourantok and tell him: 'The Bour tells you: Gather the elders on the village square, and you will give your children to the priest!' The 'Bour of the Sine' will explain later to his son what he asks of him."

"But father, why have you given all this land, our land, to the missionary?"

"Because the first day that I saw him, he spoke to me as a son to his father, so I felt like a father to him, and no matter what he would ask of me, I was going to give it to him!"

"It was an 'actual grace,'" Father Gravrand later explained to his bishop, "and I simply cooperated with it. God will bless this king. You will see: the whole kingdom of the Sine will be open to the Gospel and thus become stronger against the threat of Islam."

"I Saw How He Founds a Mission!"

The bishop returned to Diohine: he had learned of the "miracle" and wanted to follow up on it, to watch over its completion.

"Good!" he said to Father Gravrand, "what a grace! But let us go to Fatick. I will show you the place where you must build the mission!"

Father Gravrand rejoiced. In his own words:

"I saw how he was founding a mission: yard by yard, with his feet, with his legs, he surveyed the grounds. He knew that it would take so many feet by so many feet for the priests' residence, this kind of location for the church, at what distance to put the boys' school, further away for the Sisters and the girls' school, and also the workshops. And I watched him: you could tell that he had given much thought to the foundation and that it must be done just as it was in his head."

Immediately, the bishop wrote to the Superior General:

"We have made a breakthrough, send us reinforcements quickly!"

Of course, he had his African seminarians at the seminary in Palmarin. But few reached the point of studying theology.... The climate was hot and humid and not very conducive to studies. The bishop decided to move it to an oasis! Yes, an oasis in the middle of the near-desert and close to Dakar at Sambam Castle, a fairytale name, in Sébikhotane, so that the seminarians could study there in peace and almost before his eyes. He insisted on it. And he brought in young Spiritan fathers formed in Rome to rejuvenate and Romanize the faculty:

"I need 'Romans'!"

An Endless Search for Subsidies

To pay for his projects, the young bishop went in search of subsidies: either from the Pontifical Association of the Holy Childhood, whose president, Msgr. Adrien Bressolles, was known to him; or the Association for the Propagation of the Faith (of Pauline Jaricot) in Lyon; or the Sacred Congregation for the Propagation of the Faith, or the *Propaganda Fide* for short, in Rome. But sometimes it was less glamorous:

"But you have no right to this subsidy," the cashier objected, a fine, renowned ecclesiastic.

"Yes I do, since the Holy Father gave me this bill of payment to show you."

"But your diocese is rather rich! You don't need this money!"

"Yes I do, since the Holy Father recognizes that I need it."

Growing tired of the battle, the cleric in charge yielded, took out of a drawer a bundle of money and threw it across the counter, from which it fell to the ground, scattering.

And the Vicar Apostolic bent down to pick up the bills one by one: "Stay there, I'll take care of it!"

To his friend Adrien Bressolles, he explained in detail his Vicariate's needs: "When I travel through the missions, I see in the cemetery: 'Father So-and-so, arrived in 1925, died in 1929,' 'Sister So-and-so, arrived in 1927, died in 1929': dead after two years! What a slaughter! So I decided to furnish each presbytery with a refrigerator (and thus electricity), the windows with mosquito nets, each mission with an all-terrain vehicle to overcome the muck and tough sands, and also to equip the fathers and brothers with a more regular community life!"

A "Dispensary" Confronting Islam

But there were also building projects to finance. One day, when he was back from Rome, he went to see Father Jules Bourdelet, the parish priest in Bambey, another famous missionary.

"Take this, Father Jules, I have just received this donation from the Sacred Congregation for the Propagation of the Faith, enough to build a dispensary, a small bush hospital, in Ngaskop."

"In Ngaskop, Your Excellency! But you can't mean that! That group of pagan villages three leagues away from here?!"

"Yes, but it has to be built in Ngaskop!"

"At the end of an impossible trail!"

"Yes, but it has to be done in Ngaskop!"

"But think of all the cinderblocks that I'll have to transport there!"

"Yes, but Ngaskop is the place where it has to be built!"

Before the calm inflexibility of his Bishop, the missionary surrendered and impertinently exclaimed: "Oh, you stubborn old man!"

"And I could say that to *Monseigneur* Lefebvre," he said later on. "He knew his missionaries and they all obeyed him because they loved him, and when you love your boss, you want to do everything that he does."

In fact, the bishop saw the situation correctly, for in Fatick, in these villages, the "Fog Ola" would very quickly enroll in the list of pagan "Friends of the Christians," who decided to give their children to the catechist. There would be many catechumens, many baptisms. The bishop wanted to protect this region from Islamization, and he succeeded completely.

It was no surprise, then, that when Pope Pius XII set up true dioceses and a true hierarchy everywhere in Africa, he appointed Msgr. Lefebvre the first Archbishop of Dakar on September 14, 1955.

So, the new Archbishop took two measures to prepare for the future.

The Cité Catholique in Dakar

He decided first to encourage the foundation of a committee for the "Cité Catholique" in Dakar. In fact, Gérard Dubois-

Burthe, a young civil servant from the French National Institute of Statistics and Economics, arrived in 1948 to present to the Archbishop his plans to establish the work in Dakar.

"Last year," he explained, "two young men, Jean Ousset and Jean Masson, with the help of Father Jean Choulot, parish priest in Montalzat-en-Quercy, created working groups to study and promote the social kingship of Jesus Christ according to the teaching of the recent popes, especially Leo XIII and Pius XI."

"Excellent! I like that, I will consult with my priest friend, the Prior of Solesmes, Dom Georges Frénaud, who must be acquainted with your work."

And Archbishop Lefebvre promised his help in 1952 when the Cité Catholique was already under attack for being "rightist and monarchic" (*sic*), in a poorly-written article by Father Marie Joseph Nicolas, O.P., in the December 3, 1951 issue of *La Vie Spirituelle*. Time passed, and on March 17, 1957, the Archbishop of Dakar personally presided over the first public session of the Cité Catholique in his office.

Father Courrier, chaplain of Catholic Action at the Center for Charitable Works in Dakar protested in 1958: "Your Grace, this fascist organization reeks of Action Française, which influences the leadership of MP-13 in Algeria: a blight on the general good that our Catholic Action is doing!"

"What blather! Where did you hear all this? On the contrary, it promotes true social justice and concord between workers and employers!"

"But Your Grace, how then are we going to keep up our demands and our strikes, which are an opportunity to speak about Christ the liberator to the working class?"

"Now that is a curious mixture, dear Father, of Our Lord Jesus Christ and revolution! Jesus condemns such confusion by saying: 'The truth will make you free' (Jn. 8:32). And the Cité Catholique teaches this truth to the employers; so they are the ones, the economic leaders themselves, who must and will reestablish the social order and peace."

"Then there is nothing left to do but close shop. No more Catholic Action for Workers and no more Young Christian Workers!"

"I think, my dear Father, that this will not be a suppression but a reform, a true reform in the Church: I see the Cité Catholique as a nursery for the organizers of Action Catholique, as Pope Pius X envisioned it!"

And Father Courrier, horrified, withdrew in desperation.

But since this work was supported by the Spiritual Exercises of Saint Ignatius as preached to the leaders by the Parochial Cooperators of Christ the King, called "Chabeuil Fathers," Archbishop Lefebvre invited them to preach at the first retreat to his priests in Dakar. Thus Fathers Augustin Rivière and Noël Barbara came to preach two series of exercises during the winters of 1960 and 1961 to several groups of retreatants, animated by a renewed zeal for the reign of Christ the King.

Mohammed Habache, First in Catechism

The second decision the Archbishop made to prepare for the future was to build a large secondary school for boys close to Dakar, in the dunes of Hann. He constructed it to accommodate 800 students at first. It was the largest school in the country.

"Your Grace," his Vicar General Father Bussard remarked, "isn't it a little prideful? To want to build bigger schools than the State has!"

"Let's see, dear Father. There's a little virtue that Saint Thomas Aquinas calls 'magnanimity': to see things on a grand scale, to suit God! And then it's high time to rescue our young Catholics from the secularism of the State schools. The Senegal of tomorrow will be built by the alumni of this totally Catholic boarding school."

"Good, Your Grace, that's a beautiful vision! But not all our students will be Christians in this nearly entirely Muslim country!"

"We will accept the sons of Muslims, but no more than 15% of the student body, or else we will no longer be free to give a Catholic education to them all."

"At the Brothers' school, at l'École Saint-Michel, the young Mohammed Habache, who earned the highest grades in catechism, wanted to make his First Holy Communion with his friends!"

"Yes, I know his story well, he's not baptized! It's a tragedy. He has the 'baptism of desire,' does he not? But how will he persevere in his family and his whole Muslim milieu?"

"He will have to wait until he is an adult and has become independent from his family...."

"Yes, let's not despair of God's grace or of souls," said the Archbishop with faith that was still quite fresh.

CHAPTER X

Apostolic Delegate
1948-1959

"You govern the Apostolic Vicariate of Dakar so prudently, wisely and actively, you are driven by such zeal for the reign of Christ, that We judge it right to choose you to head this delegation of Ours in French Africa."

So Pius XII wrote to Archbishop Lefebvre in a Brief signed by Montini, September 22, 1948, just one year after his appointment to Dakar!

"Here I am representing the Pope to the governors of the African territories," Archbishop Lefebvre thought. "I have to go greet the High Commissioner of France to Dakar: Bernard Cornut-Gentille, even though he is a staunch Freemason."

The short visit was cordial. The Delegate remembered the directive that Father Libermann used to give to his first missionaries to Dakar: "You have to be 'on good terms' with the civil authorities, for the good of your Missions."

And Bernard Cornut-Gentille himself would be grateful for the benefit that he derived from his meetings with the Vicar and Apostolic Delegate: "Archbishop Lefebvre is the most intelligent man that I have met in Africa. And so, when he comes to see me, I am careful about what I say to him and I listen a great deal to what he is willing to confide to me."

Father Bourdelet Summoned to the Archbishop' Residence

But one day Father Jules Bourdelet is summoned by Archbishop Lefebvre to the Archbishop's residence. Being summoned by the bishop is serious business.

"Father," the prelate begins in a severe tone, "you gave a certain sermon at the cathedral on the Feast of Christ the King and ..."

Father Boudelet is not afraid. "Yes, *Monseigneur*. Did someone say that I preached false doctrine?"

"That is not the problem. I have to reprimand you...."

"Oh no, *Monseigneur!*"

"Look, I received a telephone call from the Governor General about your sermon."

"Oh, woe is me!"

"Yes, you did not pull your punches! You said: 'Even for those in civil authority who believe neither in God nor in the devil, who reject the whole supernatural realm, even in this case, their authority, in the final analysis, still comes from Christ the King, because 'all things were created by Him and in Him,' Saint Paul says (Col 1:16), even if someone rejects Him absolutely!'"

"That is indeed what I preached, *Monseigneur*. Could that be wrong?"

"No, that's not the problem."

"But what, then, *Monseigneur?*"

"It did not please the Governor General. He asked me to admonish you."

"Ah!"

"Well, then, I gave you the reprimand that I was supposed to give.... And now, Father Jules, how would it be if we took a bit of whiskey?"

That is not all: the following Sunday, the bishop is the one who ascends the pulpit and drives the message home:

"All authority comes from God, even the authority of those who deny Him!"

"My Carmelites First!"

That was well said and well done, but since the bishop was now the Delegate, he had to think about constructing a building for his Delegation. But he had to do it correctly: it was necessary to use supernatural means first; this was his apostolic motto, quite in keeping with the Gospel, according to the Lord's commandment: "Seek ye therefore first the kingdom of God and His justice: and all these things shall be added unto you" (Mt. 6:33).

"So let us go visit our Carmelites whom I sent for from Cholet, in Anjou: they are the lightning-rod of my Vicariate; they will help me in this matter."

"My dear Sisters, I received money from the Sacred Congregation of the Propagation of the Faith to build the Apostolic Delegation.... Well, with it I am going to build your Carmel! Yes, yes! To tell the truth, at the bishop's residence, when it rains, it rains on my bed! Hah! That is not important; it dries very quickly. The Delegation will come afterward."

And so it happens. And as is only right, shortly afterward the Delegate was able to build his Delegation, where he will have his office, his secretariat (Father Doutremépuich, "Father Doutre," a "Roman" was Delegation Secretary) and his apartment.

"When he goes out," Brother Christian Winckler observed, "the Archbishop likes to drive himself in his big American car, a Buick, which is representative of his office, equipped with a gold and silver pennant of the Holy See. He doesn't drive slowly, not in fits and starts either, but smoothly, just as he manages people."

And Here's a Capuchin Father, a Bishop

But his kindness was combined with firmness and sometimes with gentle shrewdness.

He had to make an emergency appointment to Berberati, in Oubangui-Chari: someone to replace Father Gabriel Tissot, a Capuchin from the Province of Savoy, who responded to his appointment to be Apostolic Prefect with a *"gran rifiuto"* [Italian:

flat refusal]. Immediately the Delegate went to visit the friaries of Savoy in search of someone capable of serving as Prefect. Father Basile Baud, the Provincial since 1948, accompanied him. They searched everywhere, without finding a suitable man.

Finally the Delegate said to himself: "This little Provincial is not so bad; he would get the job done well! The reports about him are not bad: 'Former student of the Catholic University of Lyon, he has kept the correct doctrine'; his circular letters to his Capuchin confreres recommend: 'Mary, model of the interior life and of the apostolate, community life, prayer, penance and charity.'"

Upon returning to Paris, Archbishop Lefebvre summoned the "little Provincial." The prelate energetically got right to the point: "Your subject, Father Gabriel, refuses even the position of administrator of the mission; this is serious in the Church's eyes! I see only one solution."

"I am all ears," Father Basile said unsuspectingly.

"The solution is for you, Very Reverend Father, to agree to take his place!"

Caught in the trap, the unfortunate priest did not even try to argue that he had never gone to the missions....

"I expect a favorable response on the spot," the prelate pressures the friar.

"Oh, *Monseigneur*, you got me good!"

But the Delegate had "another good turn" in store for the new Apostolic Prefect, since scarcely one year later Father Basile was appointed Vicar Apostolic of that same Berberati and therefore had to be consecrated a bishop, which took place in Annecy on June 24, 1954.

Collegiality Already!

Furthermore Delegate Lefebvre, according to orders from Rome, had to set up episcopal conferences in the various countries that report to him. He complied, but quickly gained a negative experience of these assemblies.

He asked Rome "to define their duties precisely, limit them as to their frequency and their powers, because the bishops—the very ones who by divine right have the ordinary power over their diocese—are becoming paralyzed by these assemblies."

What he himself did wonderfully was to hold a very free periodic meeting of the bishops neighboring Dakar: from Senegal, from French Guinea, from Niger and from Mauritania. Their discussions were fraternal, unforced, no "resolutions" are voted on, and every bishop remained master in his own territory.

CHAPTER XI

An Inter-Religious Ceremony in Dakar

"Passengers are asked to fasten their seat belts; we are landing in Dakar-Yoff."

Through the window of the DC 2 airliner, Archbishop Lefebvre, who was returning from the desert, Nouakchott, Mauritania, in January 1960, saw only a black, impenetrable fog. After a rather brutal shock, the plane soon was taxiing fairly well on the potholed landing strip, but on the ocean shore there was a pile of twisted metal. . . .

In the airport, where Father Duguy is waiting for him, there is the customary genuflection and kissing of the bishop's hand, in public. The Archbishop, smiling as always, does not refuse this sign of respect. But he asks: "What is that blackened heap of metal beside the runway along the ocean, dear Father?"

"Oh, *Monseigneur*, that is a plane that crashed into the water a few days ago while landing, or rather coming down onto the water, which killed 160 passengers. They still had their seat belts on; they were cut in two. They could not tell who was Catholic and who was Muslim. . . ."

Ecumenism Already!

"Yes, I heard that on the radio. But they reported a certain ceremony that is said to have taken place on the grounds adjoining the cathedral. . . ."

"*Monseigneur*, you were not there. The Director of Air France came to the bishop's residence. 'Couldn't something be done?' he asked, 'A common ceremony?' Father Bussard replied: 'Even if so,

57

not all three religions at once! I see a solution: I offer the school-yard of my primary school, next door to the bishop's residence, with its platform.' And the ceremony took place, the three religions, one after the other."

"Hmm," said the Archbishop. "I am going to see about this matter with Father Bussard...."

At the bishop's residence, after the proper greetings, the Archbishop, who was itching to speak for a change, immediately addresses his Vicar General: "Father Bussard, did you authorize that sort of multi-religious ceremony?"

"*Monseigneur*, I asked the Apostolic Nuncio, your successor, to come and give the absolution. He agreed on condition that he would do it first and would not be present for the other ceremonies. The whole government was there and several French officers."

"And then?"

"Archbishop Maury therefore gave the absolution, intoned the *Libera me*, and we Africans, who know it by heart, sang it superbly. After him came the Protestant pastor, who gave a short, bland reading; then the *marabout*."

"My God!"

"*Monseigneur*, he did not want to come. I had to ask Mamadou Dia, the Prime Minister, 'Your Excellency, I am very embarrassed. The *marabout* does not want to participate. People will think that we were unwilling to accept the participation of the Muslims, but the contrary is true!' Then he asked the *marabout*, who came to recite a few surahs from the Koran, and then that was all."

"How was that 'all'? You agreed to that?! That is *communicatio in sacris* (participation in non-Catholic worship)!"

"*Monseigneur*, the term is correct, but it does not apply: because the Catholic part was independent. And since the Apostolic Nuncio was the one who ..."

"Oh, yes, but that's nothing to go by!"

Father Bussard, who related that exchange with his Archbishop, comments: "He was gentle with everybody, but sometimes he had a little barbed comment like that."

"*Monseigneur*, no! There was no *communicatio in sacris*, no 'participation in non-Catholic worship'; and that was the triumph of the Catholics. They said: 'Truly, we were able to show the others what worship is! The others had nothing!'"

The Archbishop then turned to his secretary and friend who, according to Father Bussard, "tends to be very harsh" but in reality was a simple alumnus of Santa Chiara: "What do you think about this, Father Duguy?"

"Oh, no, *Monseigneur*, Father Bussard did right!"

"You too!"

"*Monseigneur*," Father Bussard said, "if you think that I did wrong, you know, I offer you my resignation—no problem!"

Then Archbishop Lefebvre said nothing more.

He would not have allowed this thing and cannot allow it, because of the stench of relativism or religious indifferentism entailed in the association of these three worship ceremonies, even in succession. One cannot compromise with the principles by allowing that ambiguous connection, which is equivalent to questioning the one true religion, the only one approved by God, a practical denial of the unique Mediator and Savior, Jesus Christ.

On this point Archbishop Lefebvre would never change one iota: he will say "no" to Assisi in 1986 as he did in Yoff in 1960. But he had no desire to start a debate about applying this principle: it was so clear to him and he was disconcerted to see that his most reliable collaborators had vacillated. The formula *"communicatio in sacris"* had sprung to mind because his intuitive faith, in that wave of indignation, could not find a stronger term with which to castigate the debasement of Christ and of His Church.

CHAPTER XII

An Untiring Search for New Laborers for the Gospel

"We must promote the growth of the Church in Africa," Pope Pius XII demanded, "so that it has an African clergy." Archbishop Lefebvre devoted himself to this with all his might; however, he thought, an adequate African clergy would be the product of in-depth evangelization. What he did therefore with untiring ardor and manifest success—as the Pope's Delegate from 1947 on, then from 1959 on as simple Archbishop of Dakar—was to bring to Senegal and to the other territories dependent on France new missionary or teaching congregations, many of them, in fact.

His Holy Ghost Fathers were a bit reluctant: "Careful, *Monseigneur*; this territory was assigned to us Spiritans, all the same!"

"It is true," he said, "that I am promoting a revolution, because until now one territory was reserved to one congregation: Gabon and Cameroon to the Spiritans, the Ivory Coast to the Fathers of the African Missions from Lyons, the island of Madagascar to the Jesuits, etc. But now it is time to diversify the evangelical laborers in each territory, and by that very fact to promote the establishment of true dioceses in Africa."

"To Enlist New Battalions!"

In his ceaseless quest for these new evangelical laborers in missionary lands, Archbishop Lefebvre crisscrossed Europe at the steering wheel of his Citroën registered with the license plate CD, *Corps Diplomatique.* In May-June 1955 he even traveled through French-speaking Canada at the rate of three religious or priestly houses per day. On May 24, while visiting the Trinitarians in

Montreal, he appealed to his audience of priests, brothers, scholastics and minor seminarians: "An immense harvest—four million human beings—is waiting for the divine message. Will enough laborers be found in this part of the Lord's vineyard to convert them all? Workers are needed immediately, and a lot of them."

The Delegate stopped for a moment and peers at his audience. Everyone looked expectantly into the eyes of the lecturer. And His Excellency then said: "This is the purpose of my trip to French-speaking Canada: to solicit your collaboration for the immense work of evangelizing French Black Africa."

When his lecture was over, *Monseigneur* walked toward the audience and spoke to each one. He asked the minor seminarians, who listened to him attentively, what they dreamt of being in the future.

With regard to all these Congregations that he visited and revisited on both sides of the Atlantic, Archbishop Lefebvre proved his patience and tenacity, and his conduct was governed by the watchword: "Never lose heart, keep trying!" Here he was at the major seminary in Madagascar, run by the Jesuits in Ambanidia. He arrived for his visit a bit late. After supper the students came to kiss his ring; well and good, but the Delegate would like to speak to them.

Now the Rector comes forward: "*Monseigneur*, it is time now for grand silence, so ... I'm sorry, because I know that you will leave tomorrow very early."

"Oh, it doesn't matter; I understand very well," the Archbishop replied.

He left with the same smile; but three days later, there he was again, this time at nine o'clock in the morning and without notice: "Ah! I think that now I could see your students and your instructors, we'll have plenty of time to speak before the grand silence!"

"To Form a Catholic Elite for This Muslim Country!"

In early March of 1957, the ideal time of year to enjoy the mild Roman weather before the dog days of summer, the Apostolic Delegate was in Rome, as he was every year. At the foot of the staircase that leads to the papal palace, he was greeted by the Swiss Guards who wear their multi-colored Renaissance uniform, with its crested helmet and tall halberd, just like in 1515 at the Battle of Marignan. He walked down the long corridors, where he passed one or another *Monsignore*, was led by a chamberlain into one antechamber, then into a second. A door opens, and Pope Pius XII appeared: tall, thin, ascetical, straight as an arrow, a man whom one approached only with respect and veneration.

"You're right on time, *Monseigneur* Lefebvre!" the Pontiff exclaimed in impeccable French with a slight Italian accent. "What is new in Africa?"

"Most Holy Father," the Delegate replied after genuflecting and kissing his hand, "I come to give an account of my activities...."

"Come in, please, to my private library, which belonged to my predecessor, Saint Pius X, whom I had the joy of canonizing three years ago."

"I was at the ceremony, Holy Father. My name is even inscribed in the long list of bishops who were present, engraved on the marble plaques posted at the entrance to your Basilica of Saint Peter!"

For a precisely-timed quarter of an hour, for Pius XII was brief and concise, the Delegate told about the founding of new vicariates or dioceses, the appointment of several African bishops, as auxiliary bishops at first, the multiplication of missionary or teaching Congregations, which he brought in even from Canada: "The Sacred Heart Brothers of Granby, Canada, were and are still in charge of Saint Michael's School in Dakar; I just entrusted to them the large boys' boarding school that we were able to build in the dunes of Hann, near Dakar."

"Brothers from Canada!"

"With a special railroad that I obtained from the civil authorities by insisting on it."

Pius XII smiled. He even laughed when Archbishop Lefebvre told him the story that we have heard: "We have in Dakar a young lad, son of a Muslim, who took first honors in catechism and wept on the day of First Holy Communion because he could not receive the bread of angels with his classmates."

"At least he will preserve his respect for the Catholic Church!" Pius XII said.

"Most Holy Father, that is exactly right. But you see, the purpose, the goal of our Catholic schools in these Muslim countries is different. It is to form a Catholic elite for tomorrow, so that when these countries gain independence, they may be governed by Catholic leaders and according to Catholic principles!"

Archbishop Lefebvre Rebuked, Then Encouraged by Pope Pacelli

"I understand, and I approve, *Monseigneur*.... But some have blamed you, even here in my office, for bringing to Africa a large number of priests, sisters and missionaries who are not from Africa. Doesn't this oppose the Africanization of the clergy in African that is so urgent?"

The Delegate says to himself, "Now I'm on the hot seat. It's the hour for truth!"

"No, Holy Father. We must increase as much as possible the number of Catholic battalions before the countries are made independent. With them I will form African men and women religious and an African clergy. It is a race against time! That is why I am calling so many people to Dakar."

"But some of your colleagues are a bit cramped by this influx of foreigners in your territory."

"Holy Father, on the contrary: it is enlivening and creates extraordinary emulation. My fellow bishops ask themselves: 'Why don't we do the same?'"

"Good, you reassure me," the Pope said kindly.

"Look at the statistics of the Delegation. ..."

Pius XII liked maps and numbers; he pored attentively over those of the Delegate. The latter concluded his demonstration victoriously: "We must evangelize these countries as much as possible, so that they will one day resist the Muslim pressure and the Communist slavery that threaten them!"

Upon returning to Dakar, Archbishop Lefebvre could say to Father Duguy, the new secretary of the Delegation: "Pope Pius XII is capable of understanding me and of supporting us!"

This was true. The Delegate had just left Pius XII when the Pontiff received another visitor, telling him, "Do you see the prelate who just left here?"

"Yes, Holy Father. Who is it?"

"Archbishop Lefebvre, my best Apostolic Delegate!"

Confronting the Future Pope Paul VI

But at the Sacred Congregation for the Propagation of the Faith, the overly enterprising Delegate was met instead with a lack of understanding and hostility. The Secretary of the Congregation, Archbishop Celso Costantini, said to whoever will listen: "White missionaries are not going to Christianize Africa, no! The black priests are the ones who will do it. And those black priests will then come to Europe to Christianize us!"

When someone related these remarks to him, Archbishop Lefebvre exclaims, "That a high-ranking prelate in the Curia, an Archbishop, who of all things is in charge of the propagation of the faith, should thus ignore and despise the work of the missionaries is unimaginable!"

In the Autumn of 1957, in Rome, Archbishop Lefebvre was again at the Vatican, received this time at the Secretariat of State by Archbishop Montini, the future Pope Paul VI, one of the two "Substitutes" because Pius XII holds the office of Secretary of State.

"*Monsignore*," the Delegate asked him, "could the Holy See warn against a movement that is doing harm in Africa, the 'Moral Rearmament'? It invites politicians, even Catholics, to sessions in Caux, above Vevey in Switzerland, for the purpose of universal fraternity among men of all religions. It is a crypto-Masonic organization!"

"Oh, no, no, no! The Church must not always condemn, condemn, condemn. She will look like a wicked stepmother!"

Back in Dakar, he told Father Duguy, his new secretary at the Delegation: "I got nothing, not even a warning. Nothing! As much as Archbishop Tardini, the other Substitute of the Secretariat, is firm, courageous, a man of the Church, Archbishop Montini is just as fleeting, vague, fearful of combat and difficulties...."

Archbishop Lefebvre Dismissed by John XXIII

Alas, the great Pope Pacelli would die in 1958, and his successor, John XXIII, who could be swayed by the liberal illusions circulating in the Curia, took away Archbishop Lefebvre's responsibility as Apostolic Delegate (1959).

"Here. A letter from the Secretariat of State."

Archbishop Lefebvre read:

"Your Excellency, the Holy Father John XXIII offers you the choice between keeping the Archdiocese of Dakar or the Apostolic Delegation. ... Signed Cicognani."

"They put it in such kindly terms! Father Duguy, write my reply: Your Most Reverend Eminence, I will not choose; I am not the one who appointed myself Archbishop or Apostolic Delegate. Let the Holy Father choose!"

One month later, while Archbishop Lefebvre was spending three days in Pech-Petite, a calm villa in the Basque Country at the home of his brother Joseph, a second missive from the Secretariat of State arrived.

"Your Excellency, since you have expressed a preference for the Archdiocese of Dakar, the Holy Father deigns to discharge you from the office of Apostolic Delegate."

"What is this?" asked Joseph Lefebvre.

"Oh, it's nothing. I am no longer Apostolic Delegate...."

He felt the pain cruelly. He needed to pray. He withdrew to his room. That evening he reappeared at supper, calm again. He even explained the Roman "gentle cunning": "I had not expressed any preference. But that is the Roman way of doing things!"

And John XXIII ended up taking away his position as Archbishop of Dakar too (1961).

It is true that Leopold Senghor, President of the young Republic of Senegal, complained to the Vatican about the public letter dated March 26, 1961, written by the Archbishop on the subject of the "African socialism" of the President and entitled "On the Duty to Live According to the Truth and to Avoid Ambiguities." Here, in effect, is what Archbishop Lefebvre said in it:

"Some claim to be inspired by socialism while denying its atheism, hoping thereby to make it more compatible with the Church's doctrine. But in accepting the word (socialism), they nonetheless swallow the thing whole! It is not enough to profess faith in God; it is necessary to recognize that God is the foundation of the law, and not the State. A State that suppresses all private initiatives, and then to manage them requires a monstrous bureaucracy that takes possession of all the wealth of intellect, art, the spirit of enterprise, invention, and charity, in order to nationalize them and dry them up!"

Leopold, shocked by these truths administered too sharply by the prelate, let the Vatican know that the latter could say them better in France. And Pope John gave in; besides, it was his intention to appoint an African bishop to Dakar.

Therefore he appointed Archbishop Lefebvre Bishop of Tulle, a poor little diocese in France, not even to the Archdiocese of Albi which was vacant then. In reality, the cardinals and Archbishops of France took necessary steps along these lines with the Holy See in November 1961 and even with the French government in January 1962: "Above all, don't let Archbishop Lefebvre be appointed to an archdiocese, so that he will not be a member of the Assembly of Cardinals and Archbishops."

They fear "this Lefebvre" [there was at that time another French prelate by the same name], "who is notorious for his fundamentalist tendencies and his open promotion of *Verbe*, the magazine of the Cité Catholique movement."

Archbishop Lefebvre commented tranquilly on the pettiness: "Saint Francis de Sales says that one soul is worth a diocese. Well, then, in Tulle, I will have a large diocese!"

CHAPTER XIII

The Cité Catholique, the French Bishops and Pope John XXIII

Even before making his first contacts with Tulle, the Archbishop resided in Paris, at the General House of the Holy Ghost Fathers, 30 rue Lhomond, in the "Latin Quarter," two steps away from the Pantheon, the old Saint Genevieve Church. In November 1961, Father Matthew Farelly, the sympathetic Secretary General of the Spiritans, called his attention to the public attacks in the press against his friends in the Cité Catholique movement.

The Art of Thwarting a Scheme

"*Monseigneur*, this is a 'leak': these are excerpts from a 'Confidential Note,' in other words, a secret document addressed to the French episcopate, about Jean Ousset's organization!"

"Say, rather, 'an article from the leading core group of the episcopate'! And what does it say?"

"Here, *Monseigneur*, I quote it verbatim: 'In the Cité Catholique, systematized ways of thinking end up stifling reflection. Its members ceaselessly quote the magisterial documents of the popes but without knowing how to interpret them. They try to sacralize the temporal order without respecting its correct autonomy from the spiritual order. They try to silence the movements that demand social justice. The shrewdness of the themes of the magazine *Verbe* sterilizes the movements of Catholic Action.'"

"This is a coup that they're staging," the Archbishop says immediately, "a plot to oblige the Assembly of Cardinals and Archbishops to issue a warning against the Cité Catholique."

"*Monseigneur*, how do you know that?"

"Remember the condemnation of Action Française! In 1926, Rome had succeeded in persuading Cardinal Andrieu, Archbishop of Bordeaux, to accuse Maurras' movement of atheism and paganism! So that Pope Pius XI could intervene and get rid of those monarchists who were hampering his policy of rapprochement with the Masonic government of the French Republic!"

"Oh, you know, *Monseigneur*, we Englishmen aren't familiar with those old quarrels!"

"Old quarrels? But don't you see that today it's the same tactic on the part of the Church authorities in France with regard to a movement which this time is quite Catholic but hampers the revolutionary Action Catholique? It is the technique of defamatory labeling and exclusion, a Communist technique!"

"I see, *Monseigneur*. All the same, you are not going to intervene, are you?"

"I am going to block their business immediately. There has to be one bishop who breaks solidarity with them, and I'll be the one. Note this down: I am going to dictate to you my letter of support to Jean Ousset; date it March 4, 1962:

'Dear Monsieur Ousset, do they reproach you for not having all the episcopal approvals? They are not absolutely required for your activity, which is not their sort of Catholic Action. Do they reproach you for undermining Catholic Action? But you are the one who is conducting it as Pope Pius X wanted it: to fight against anti-Christian society! Do they reproach you for not knowing how to interpret the Encyclicals of the popes? Above all beware of interpreting them as they do; that would be to deprive papal documents of all their authority! Do they reproach you for teaching the doctrine of Christ the King? But this is the Church's doctrine, that of Pope Saint Pius X, of Pope Pius XI, of Pope Pius XII and again recently of Cardinal Ottaviani in Rome.'"

"Well said, *Monseigneur*!"

"And you will send a copy of this letter, dear Father, to the newspapers *Le Monde* and *Rivarol*!"

And soon there was a fine hullabaloo among the French bishops and in the press. In the progressive Catholic newspaper *La Croix* (which people have called "*The Cross* without a cross" ever since the disappearance of the cross of Christ which used to adorn the first page), the editors were beating around the bush. The issue dated March 16, 1962, elicited the responses of Jean Madiran— more like a bullfighter's *banderillas*—in his magazine *Itinéraires*, nos. 61, 62, 64 and 66. But that is not all.

John XXIII Teaches Archbishop Lefebvre a Lesson

On May 7, Archbishop Lefebvre was, as they put it politely, "received in audience" by Pope John XXIII, who for an hour taught him a lesson in his own way:

"You see," said Good Pope John, "when I was a professor of Sacred Scripture in Bergamo, I supported the theses of Father Marie-Joseph Lagrange. A fatal false step! I was labeled a 'Modernist'; that harmed me my whole life long. Recently I decided to look at my file; I read: 'Modernist tendency ...' No! I am not a Modernist! And because of that, I was never appointed to Rome, they always kept me far from the Roman Curia because—they said—I was a Modernist! Well, *Monseigneur*, you should be careful not to label yourself in a similar way as a conservative."

Upon his return from Rome, the Archbishop related the papal admonition.

"There," he said to Father Farelly in conclusion, "that is how Pope John XXIII admonished me, 'be prudent if you want to advance your career'! But I don't care about advancing my career!"

"But, *Monseigneur*, weren't you almost made a cardinal?"

"Ah, so you got wind of that story!"

"Tell us!"

"Under Pius XII the rumor circulated that they were going to offer me the red hat; my aunt, Madame Lemaire, was the one who absolutely wanted me to be a cardinal, and so she took steps along those lines, if you see what I mean.... In doing so, she scuttled the matter. The red hat passed right by, like a flying saucer. Luckily! Otherwise, I would never have been appointed to Tulle!"

CHAPTER XIV

Hope for a Diocese in Danger
Tulle – 1962

"You heat the place with this gas stove?"

"Yes, *Monseigneur*," the poor priest replied, "and what's more, I have to pay back the car that the diocese gave me."

At the rectory of a quaint, remote corner of Corrèze, the young curate of Recoules-Gayrac confided even more frankly in his new bishop: "*Monseigneur*, I was assigned here. But what good am I doing? On Sundays there are only four or five old ladies at Mass, and almost no children at catechism class. And then I am alone."

"Listen to me. Prepare your daily Mass. Take great care. It has to be perfect. Let all the gestures prescribed by the rubrics express your faith, your devotion. You have nothing personal to put into the rite, but rather your heart into the sacred action. The fruit of a single Mass celebrated by a good priest in unimaginable. Think of the saintly Curé of Ars. After you have celebrated your Mass in this way, you will have accomplished 80% of your apostolate! Moreover, through us priests it is Our Lord who acts; we are only poor instruments. He who tells himself this is armed against discouragement if the apostolate is unsuccessful."

"Nothing is Lost!"

The Archbishop was back at the bishop's residence, a modest low concrete building with a little parking lot and a few trees, alongside the road from Tulle to Égletons. It was ugly and poor but functional. He told Msgr. Layotte, his chancellor, about his visit to the de-Christianized village of Monédières; it was heart-

73

wrenching; but he optimistically confided: "Nothing is desperate here; several ideas occur to me, I have my plan!"

At the first meeting of deans, he proposed: "What if the bishop came to visit his priests where they live, in their rectory? To get acquainted with them and to know their difficulties."

"Oh, *Monseigneur*," exclaimed the curate from Laroch-Canillac who spoke his mind, "You tell us that but you will do as the others did; we will not see you!"

"Reverend Father, do you have a date book with which to schedule an appointment?"

"I must have a slip of paper somewhere...."

The date was set, and soon the episcopal Citroën 2CV, driven by the Archbishop-Bishop of Tulle under a roof that flapped in the wind, braked with a squeak in front of the humble rectory. The little old car stopped and swayed on its suspension.

"Ah, Reverend Father, so you are all alone here, isolated! That will not continue! I will regroup you with several priests per house, and you will run a school, and you will also drive the school bus! Thus we will revive our Catholic primary schools. And in Brive, I will create another secondary boarding school for Catholic boys. And from it we will have vocations, and I will reopen my seminary, which was closed by Bishop Chassaigne! And we will have new young Christian homes!"

"And for the girls ...?"

"Preach about the religious vocation; and if you see some pious young ladies, bring them together in a pious charitable association; there you will find vocations. I will revive the Congregation of the Nursing Sisters of Lacabane; they will also teach the children. Nothing is lost, quite the contrary!"

Bishop on the Ground

One day in 1962, at the bishop's residence, Msgr. Layotte called to his ordinary: "The prison in Tulle holds the officers who started the uprising in Algiers on April 22, 1961, who tried to keep Algeria French."

"What if I went to visit them?"

"Go ahead, *Monseigneur*; they deserve it and they are neglected."

Alas, two weeks later: "I just received answers from the Ministry of the Armed Forces and from the Ministry of the Interior; they say *nyet*! How happy I would be to speak personally to those heroes! Make sure to find an understanding chaplain for them."

What might this prelate, full of faith and of the love of Jesus Christ, have accomplished if he had not been elected, on July 1, 1962, successor to Father Francis Griffith as the head of the Congregation of the Holy Ghost!

This certainly was the opinion of Msgr. Meyssignac, his Vicar-General: "Of the eight bishops that I have known successively in Tulle, he, Archbishop Lefebvre, is the one who best met the qualifications of a bishop. On the ground he was 'formidable.' He was Bishop of Tulle for just six months; he spent only thirty-one days in the diocese. But in Tulle he was an excellent bishop 'on the ground' with an extraordinary presence, and a bishop very close to his priests. I say that because it is the truth, even though it doesn't please everyone!"

Meanwhile the Archbishop would bring this truth of Our Lord Jesus Christ and of the Church to the Council. . . .

CHAPTER XV

Confronting the Conciliar Deviations

Big flakes of snow were falling in Tulle, in February 1962, with a wind strong enough to uproot the most solid oaks. The Archbishop-Bishop looked at the gusts through the window of the bishop's residence: "Brr, for me this is a change from the torrid head of Senegal!"

He saw the postman and he himself walked down to the mailbox of his residence. "Look, an envelope from the Holy See! Could it be announcing a new, even more serious storm?"

Having been appointed in 1960 to the Central Preparatory Commission for Vatican Council II, Archbishop Lefebvre had to examine its schemas, its rough drafts, we might say.

He decided to open the large letter stamped *"Città del Vaticano."* He was skimming its contents when his Chancellor, Msgr. Layotte, his fellow student at Santa Chiara Seminary, came into his office. The bishop handed him the document: "Here, look. This is an excellent schema: the one of chapter IX on the Church: *On the relations between the Church and the State and religious tolerance*! This is Catholic doctrine: the State can only tolerate, within certain limits, the false religions so as to avoid a situation of war between religions. Right?"

"That is indeed what we learned at the seminary. Who wrote this schema?"

"The Commission on Theology headed by Cardinal Ottaviani. But look, another schema that is attached to the first: this one by the Secretariat for the Unity of Christians, by Cardinal Bea. What right does this 'Secretariat' have to present a schema?"

"And what does it say?"

"Exactly the opposite. 'Religious liberty' is what the State ought to recognize for the adherents of all religions, in the name of freedom of conscience. This is incredible."

"In fact, Popes Gregory XVI, Pius IX and Leo XIII explicitly condemned that proposition."

"So now we find the rights of man and the 1789 French Revolution in a conciliar schema! This is unimaginable!"

"*Monseigneur*, will you intervene on this subject?"

"Yes, certainly! At one of the next preparatory sessions."

"It is quite clear, *Monseigneur*, that every human being must follow his conscience, provided that it is true, or at least, if it is wrong, that it be without fault on his part, as is the case with many Muslims or Buddhists."

"But that they should have the right publicly, in society, to practice their religion, even in good conscience, that is quite another matter, and that is not true!"

"*Monseigneur*, this is indeed what dear Father Le Floch taught us in Rome: The truth alone and those who are in the truth have the natural right to practice the religion of God, which is specifically the religion of Our Lord Jesus Christ and of the Church."

"But in some circumstances, the State can tolerate within certain limits the worship services of false religions. This is not a 'natural right' of these persons; it is only a form of tolerance. There you have it!"

"Even though this tolerance is becoming general in our time, isn't it just a 'civil right' conceded by civil law? And not a 'natural right'?"

"That is indeed what I am going to recall at a future meeting, in Rome!"

Toward Liturgical Anarchy

Archbishop Lefebvre was therefore in Rome, at the Palace of the Sacred Office, where the preparatory session of March-April

1962 was taking place. At it, a schema by Father Bugnini on a systematic reform of the liturgy was presented.

"This schema is the most remarkable of all," declared Cardinal Döpfner, Archbishop of Munich. And the liberal Cardinals Lercaro, Montini, Alfrink, Frings, König and Liénart chime in.

"No," replied Cardinal Ottaviani, "that is such a pile of changes that there seems to be a revolutionary reform, which will cause scandal among the Christian people!"

Cardinals Browne, Siri and Ruffini commented along these lines also.

"The liturgy is incorrectly defined," Archbishop Lefebvre explained, "because sanctification occurs first through adoration, through the worship rendered to God, which are acts of the virtue of religion!"

"And then," added Father Paul Philippe (a member of the Roman Curia), "concelebration will diminish the number of Masses: the fruit of a concelebrated Mass is less than that of several Masses celebrated by each priest."

"As for the vernacular instead of Latin in the Mass," Archbishop Lefebvre then said, *"non placet.* I don't like it! Here is my position, based on my missionary experience: The indigenous priests of Africa have refused to have the *Kyrie,* the *Gloria* and the *Credo* translated into the local languages: all the faithful know these chants by heart and know that the Latin language is a sign and a guarantee of unity in faith."

He continued his argument by relating a concrete fact, as he knew how to do to support his reasoning: this is the "practical lesson": "During the Pan-African Congress in Dakar, the presidents of the civil governments, Senghor from Senegal, Tsirana from Madagascar, Maga from Dahomey, and Yaméogo from Upper Volta, gathered at the cathedral for Solemn Mass, themselves sang, in unison and in a loud voice, the Latin chants, including the *Gradual*; and after the Mass they told us that the rejoiced in that unanimity!"

And the Archbishop drove the point home by denouncing the consequences of having versions of the rites in the vernacular: "If the Holy See leaves it up to the Episcopal Conferences to establish their versions of the rites in their languages, there will be a true regression of the liturgy toward national rites; two centuries of efforts, thanks to Dom Guéranger, to promote liturgical unity will evaporate; art and sacred music will fall into ruins. There is danger of anarchy!"

A Tragic Altercation

June 19, 1962, arrived. An overwhelming heat stifled Rome; they had reached the last preparatory session, again at the Holy Office. All the preparatory schemas had been examined; the last two were on the green tablecloth of the long table where the cardinals and bishops are sitting: the duty of the State toward the true religion, according to Tradition, and next to it the duty of the State toward the false religions, according to liberalism! Two contradictory doctrines!

Archbishop Lefebvre was floored: he was witnessing an altercation between two cardinals: "A tragic confrontation," he said.

Ottaviani stood up first and spoke indignantly without beating around the bush. "It is necessary to eliminate the schema of the Secretariat for Unity," he said, "It smacks too much of contacts with non-Catholics! It is necessary to set forth undisputed Catholic doctrine!"

"But," said Bea, standing up immediately, "the non-Catholics blame the Church for being intolerant when she is in power and for demanding religious liberty for herself when she is in the minority. Where is the logic? Every sincere man must be left free to follow his conscience!"

"Freedom of conscience in the external, public forum," Archbishop Lefebvre murmured, "that's just crazy!"

When Marcel Lefebvre stood up in turn, he pronounces a *non placet* (I do not approve): "This 'religious liberty' is founded on false principles that have been solemnly rejected by the Supreme Pontiffs, who call freedom of conscience and of religion 'insanity.'"

And with regard to Ottaviani: "On the other hand, I like the competing schema, *placet*. This is the doctrine of the public right of the Church: only Catholics have an absolute, certain and unlimited right to religious liberty; the non-Catholics have only an abstract, precarious and presumed—*existimatum*—right to practice their religion. This right must yield to the certain right of Catholics: *praesumptio cedat veritati*, says the legal axiom, 'let the presumption yield to the truth.' In any case the religion of non-Catholics can be tolerated in certain circumstances for the sake of public peace."

"But," he added, "the presentation of the Catholic principles should underscore Christ the King, apart from whom there is no salvation, neither for individuals nor for nations; this is what Pius XI teaches in *Quas primas*!"

A man full of the spirit of wisdom had just stood up against the apostasy of the nations, of a liberal and Masonic nature, which the Council could not ratify without depriving itself of the assistance of the Holy Spirit....

CHAPTER XVI

Organizer of the "Battle" 1962-1965

It was October 11, 1962. The rain that had soaked Rome for two days had stopped; the clouds had parted to reveal a radiant sun. Six by six, the 2,600 Council Fathers, bishops in cope and miter, entered Saint Peter's Basilica, split up to the right and to the left and climbed into high bleachers set up on either side of the nave. Pope John XXIII then made his entrance.

Aggiornamento: the Church Suited to Today's Taste

In his speech, John rebuked the "prophets of doom" who announced the end of the world (he was referring to the third part of the secret of Fatima which he had read) and declared that "The Church must stop condemning errors, since reason itself rejects them," and that She "must offer teaching of a pastoral sort, in other words, expressed in the language of modern thought."

At the break, Archbishop Lefebvre asked his Spiritan confrere, Archbishop Alvez del Pinho, Archbishop of Luanda in Angola: "Didn't the Councils always have the purpose of condemning errors and warning against contemporary thought?"

"Yes, *Monsenhor*, and the French Cardinal Pie says that 'The Church never highlights her truth better than when she condemns the contrary errors'!"

"And expressing the faith in terms of modern thought? If the thought is idealist, wouldn't that be suppressing the faith? Look at Kant and his *Religion Within the Limits of Reason Alone*; look at Loisy and his *Life of Jesus*—a Jesus who is merely a somewhat more human man!"

"Ah, *Monsenhor*, although the *aggiornamento* (adapting the Church to the tastes of the day) desired by the Holy Father consists of adapting the faith to the method of modern thought, shouldn't the Magisterium (the Church's teaching authority) do the opposite: adapt human thought to the Word of God (Heb. 11:3)? Otherwise it would deprive the Council of the assistance of the Holy Spirit from the start!"

Indeed, following the Pope's speech, a French satirical newspaper, *Le Canard enchaîné* (*The Chained Duck*, although unchained that day) published a cartoon: in it we see the Council Fathers at the café at Saint Peter's, smoking up a storm with their cigars and cigarettes, and the dove of the Holy Ghost in the form of an airplane; the pilot says in a "balloon": "Visibility zero; landing impossible!"

The Reaction Organizes

And behold the Council voted on a "Message to the World": "Let us reach an understanding with the world, let us work together to make a more human, more fraternal humanity!"

The Archbishop intervened in the Aula: "This text is full of naturalism and purely human ideals!"

Immediately afterward, a small, thin bishop with intelligent eyes sparkling behind his thick glasses approached Archbishop Lefebvre: "Ah, *Monsenhor*, I congratulate you on your intervention! Eye em," he says with a Portuguese accent, "beeshop of a leetle Brahzeeleean diocese, Campos; my name is Antônio de Castro Mayer."

"Ah! I read your pastoral letter on 'The Problems of the Modern Apostolate' with your 'Catechism of Opportune Truths' published by the Cité Catholique, in which you follow the Church's Magisterium and do the opposite of all the current liberal ideas: What a delight! Finally, I meet you!"

"Allow me to introduce to you ... Eh! Dom Geraldo, come here! ... *Monsenhor*, this is His Excellency Geraldo de Proença Sigaud, my friend from São Paulo, Bishop of Jacarezinho. The three of us could organize a 'little committee' against the modernist and liberal forces that are ready to lay siege to the Council."

"Good idea! I can be 'the cover' as Superior General of the Spiritans; you can be in charge of 'the ideas' and Msgr. Sigaud can 'direct operations.' And we will have a 'columnist': Msgr. Carli, Bishop of Segni in Italy. And we will invite a few other bishops with a fighting spirit. My friend from Santa Chiara, Father Berto, can be a good secretary, and Dom Frénaud, a monk at Solesmes, will be a reliable doctrinal support. Father Abbot will 'lend' him to me."

"But how are we to publicize our reflections and our voting recommendations?"

"I'll take charge of that," Archbishop Lefebvre replies. "First we'll draw up a list of solid Fathers who have the Roman spirit; then Cardinal Larraona will put two Claretian priests at our disposal and even typewriters and photocopy machines."

"What about distribution? Our young men from the Brazilian T.F.P. [Tradition, Family and Property] can manage it! But we will need an automobile."

"I place at their disposal the Peugeot 203 of our General House in Rome; they will go discreetly at night delivering our letters to the Fathers' places of residence."

And so it would be done....

Never the Policy of Pessimism!

Twenty-five years later, the seminarians in Ecône would question Archbishop Lefebvre: "*Monseigneur*, what was the influence of the *Coetus*, that group of bishops who joined the resistance with you during the Council?"

"We limited the damage, without being able to purify the Council of the liberal spirit that imbued it. When a document is composed in a wrong spirit, it is impossible to expurgate it. You would have to rewrite it entirely according to the Catholic spirit. Through the *modi* [proposed revisions] that we presented, we were able to interpolate some clauses that tone down the errors, but they remain like foreign bodies in texts that are basically wrong-headed."

"Would it not have been preferable to leave the texts completely wrong in their approach?"

"I have never been in favor of the policy of pessimism. Look, at the end of the first session of the Council, our friend Bishop Adam of Sion in Switzerland told me: 'I am not coming back to the second session.' I said to him: 'Do stay, and fight inch by inch with us!' 'The Holy Ghost has deserted the Council; I too can leave it....' That was his style. And so he did not come back, and after the Council, he let everything go in his diocese; he was desperate."

"And you, *Monseigneur*, you stayed?"

"But of course; I felt driven to intervene; out of fidelity to the heritage that I had received in Santa Chiara I wanted to fight: for example, to save the primacy of the Pope (the superior or supreme authority of the Pope over the bishops) in spite of the Pope!"

But I ought to tell the story of the battles of the *Coetus*.

CHAPTER XVII

The Battles of the Coetus
at the Council

The *"piccolo comitato"* [Italian: "little committee"], gathered around Archbishop Lefebvre, grew during the third session of the Council into a group of 250 Council Fathers. But what would it be called? Archbishop Lefebvre proposed: "Let us simply name it *Coetus Internationalis Patrum*: 'International Group of Fathers'; it is neutral, but it will frighten the liberal Council Fathers."

"It will even alarm the Holy Father," remarked Father Berto.

"And to think that in fact it is just a simple list without formal membership or any sort of organization!"

Stop Collegiality!

"Our first battle," Archbishop Lefebvre explains, "is against collegiality."

Dino Staffa, a Curial Archbishop, was invited to explain what that is. He says: "Here, the schema on the Church, in number 22, says this: 'Not only the Pope, the successor of Peter, has the supreme and plenary power of government over the whole Church, but the episcopal body or «episcopal college,» under its head, the Pope, also has this plenary power over all the Church.'"

"But is this a heresy?" asked Msgr. Carli.

"No," Archbishop Lefebvre intervened, "but it seems to me to be an error. The bishops do not have the habitual power of governing the whole Church with the Pope! Now this is the power that the liberals want to see declared by the Council: a sort of episcopal democracy!"

"Then what is the truth that we must set forth?"

"You know very well," Archbishop Lefebvre spoke again. "What does happen takes place at Ecumenical Councils: when the Pope approves the decisions of the Council Fathers, he gives to them, through this approval, a share in his supreme and plenary power. That's all!"

"But *Monseigneur*," the Father Abbot of Solesmes, Dom Jean Prou spoke up, "doesn't the *'Explanatory Note'* which the Holy Father has just made them add to the document correct the error of collegiality?"

"No, Most Reverend Father," Msgr. Carli replied, "it only limits it. The *Note* maintains that the College of bishops has the power to govern the whole Church with the Pope; but it explains that the College exercises this power only 'at intervals' and 'with the consent of its Head,' which avoids heresy and safeguards the dogma of papal primacy."

"However," Archbishop Lefebvre added, with his concrete sense of things, "the bishops can still complain that the Pope is exercising the supreme power alone without them, they can demand to exercise it with him! The Council will say that they are right. That is the error!"

Confronting Liberal Maneuvers
to Save Communism

At the next session, Msgr. Sigaud was uneasy: "What happened to our petition to get the Council to condemn Communism?"

Archbishop Lefebvre replied: "I myself brought to the Secretariat of the Council our petition signed by 332 Fathers, which now has collected 454 signatures. But the reporter (the one who reports to the others the corrections made to the schemas) of the schema on *The Church in the World* continues to remain silent about Communism. Let us lodge a complaint with the Secretariat of the Council."

And two days later, Archbishop Lefebvre assembled the core group of the *Coetus*. "Here, in short, is the response from the

Secretariat: the petition was 'unfortunately mislaid' in a drawer of the Commission responsible for the schema! I therefore suspect Msgr. Glorieux, Secretary of the Commission. And someone told me that it is now too late to take our petition into account!"

"And so," Father Berto said, "the Council will in practice remain silent about the most colossal 'sign of the times': the practice of dialectical materialism and the enslavement of the masses as a system of government, as Jean Madiran shows in his book, *The Age of the World: an Essay on Communism*. Now these are the diabolical techniques of the Communists in Russia, in China, in Cuba, etc."

Marriage: Human Love First, and Then Children?

At the same session, Father Berto asked Archbishop Lefebvre: "Will you intervene about the 'two ends' of marriage? The traditional doctrine is that the first end, in other words, the first purpose of marriage is 'the transmission of life and the raising of children' and the second end is 'the mutual support of the spouses and a remedy to concupiscence' (remedy to disordered sexual attraction): that is true realism! Now Archbishop Leo Suenens of Malines claims that we should reverse the two ends: first would come 'human love' and only then children."

"This inversion is serious indeed," the Archbishop replied. "First, the Church has never spoken about 'human love'! And if 'love' is placed first, someone could say: 'No love, therefore not a true marriage!' Now how many marriages are contracted quite validly without what they want to call love!"

"And isn't the best proof of true love to make a commitment forever in the bonds of one indissoluble union, a union that nothing can dissolve, break or destroy?"

"That is quite right. But I would say, more seriously, to put 'human love' or 'the good of the spouses' first, while demoting the transmission of life, is to open the door to contraception and abortion, or even to more vile things!"

True Religious Liberty: That of Catholic Worship!

At the third session of the Council, the schema on religious liberty was rejected for the third time. On October 9, 1964, Cardinal Bea had to read in the Aula, "by the order of a superior," in other words, as ordered by Pope Paul VI, that the scheme will be "recast" by a commission of four Fathers, including ... Archbishop Lefebvre!

"Magnificent, *Monseigneur!*" Antonio de Castro Mayer said to his friend, "your name unleashed a gale of panic in the ranks of the liberal Fathers! They met with Cardinal Frings, Archbishop of Cologne, to beg the Pope 'urgently, very urgently' to reform that commission, 'the composition of which causes the greatest dismay'!"

"It's done," Archbishop Lefebvre replied calmly. "I just learned that my name has been crossed off! I frighten them...."

But the issue of religious liberty returned to the agenda in the fourth session: on November 18, 1965, the *Coetus* sent to the 800 Fathers two dense pages of solid doctrine:

"Even though freedom of conscience has been toned down, the schema must be rejected: religious liberty now is supposedly based on 'the dignity of the human person' which is said to consist of 'being left free of all pressure or threat which would prevent one from practicing religion externally in society according to one's conscience.'"

"And that is false," said Marcel Lefebvre to his friends in the core group of the *Coetus*, "a person's freedom does not consist of leaving him free to believe and to publish his fables or to render false worship to God or worship to a false god, but to be prevented from doing so!"

"Yes," Father Berto emphasized, "the true dignity of the human person, as Leo XIII teaches, does not consist in the liberty to err or to sin, but in the liberty to think and to say what is true and to do what is good! That is found in his encyclical *Libertas* from 1888."

"But does that mean, in your opinion," objects Msgr. de la Chanonie, a bit frightened, "that the non-Catholics have no right to practice their religion?"

"Externally, no right. Unless for reasons of keeping the peace, the State, at the Church's judgment, decides to grant some tolerance to the false religions and to guarantee it by a *civil right*. Leo XIII teaches that freedom of religion 'is not a right that *nature* gives to man.'"

"Oh, I wasn't familiar with this document!"

"It appears also in his encyclical *Libertas*."

"We have to understand correctly," Msgr. Carli intervened, "the difference between a *natural right* that is valid for all and always because of human nature, and a *civil right*, which is valid because of circumstances, according to civil law. You have to be able to make distinctions so as to avoid saying stupid things."

Alas, finally, on December 7, 1965, the false religious liberty was proclaimed by Paul VI at the closing session of the Council: the objections of the *Coetus* were not considered.

"To the very end," Archbishop Lefebvre said, "seventy Fathers, including Msgr. de Castro Mayer and myself, voted 'No' to religious liberty. A renowned expert on constitutional law considered this number significant enough to cast doubt on the authority of *Dignitatis humanae*."

Dom Prou looked at the Archbishop quizzically, "But you signed that document after all!"

"Yes, because the Pope promulgated it. I could not separate myself from the Pope! And then Paul VI might give it a correct interpretation. But I remain convinced that the conciliar religious liberty is a doctrinal error. Isn't it, along with collegiality and ecumenism, the application to the Church of the Masonic motto of the three liberal 'values': liberty, equality, fraternity? You see, in the government of my dear Congregation of the Holy Ghost, I apply as often as possible the true motto: Truth, hierarchy, paternity."

CHAPTER XVIII

Superior General of the Spiritans 1962-1968

The General Chapter of the Spiritans (Holy Ghost Fathers) commenced in July 1962 in Chevilly, to the south of Paris, on a beautiful wooded property, with large buildings that form the theological scholasticate (or seminary) of the Congregation.

A Turbulent Election

From the start, frictions were evident between the capitulants (members of the meeting which is called the Chapter) concerning Archbishop Lefebvre, whom some would like as Superior General to restore order, and whom others do not want at all.

"*Monseigneur*, a group of fathers, all progressives, give this advice: 'Vote for whomever you like, but not for Msgr. Lefebvre!'"

"Oh, that doesn't bother me. Anyway, I do not hide my intentions: If I am elected, I will clean up Chevilly!"

The Archbishop was elected Superior General on July 26 and was installed on the 28th, after the approval of the election by Pope John XXIII.

Since the death of Pius XII and the arrival of Pope John, a wind of reform had started to blow at the scholasticate in Chevilly, among the superior and his professors of Sacred Scripture, liturgy and theology.

"*Monseigneur*," said Father Jean Letourneur, Procurator General, "the Rule of the Congregation assigns to the Superior General the duty of watching over 'sound doctrine.'"

"I do know that, dear Father, but you know that wisdom and custom require that I wait a year, or at least six months, before acting."

Here, then, were his decisions dated April 1963:

"I ask the superiors of the scholasticates to remove from their teaching positions all who are imbued with modernist ideas. We must avoid everything that minimizes the historical truth of the Scriptures, the value of Tradition, the fundamental notions of sin and personal responsibility; and prevent the invasion of the spirit of the world into our religious communities. It is absolutely necessary to avoid debating with the scholastics the essential points of discipline and of their studies. The custom of using the familiar form of address (*tu*), which has been introduced among the confreres, is regrettable. In the liturgy we follow the regulations from Rome. Explanations of the rites given during the ceremonies must be brief. In our scholasticates, the Mass will be celebrated facing the people only by way of exception."

"That is clear and neat, dear *Monseigneur*," says Father Hack; "many of our confreres appreciate the strength of your principles and the simplicity of your directives."

"Yes, that is indeed what I observe," replies Father Bernard Aguillon, one of the secretaries of the Spiritan General House, who confides to a confrere: "What a Superior he is! Kind, welcoming, listening, straightforward. It is a blessing to work with him. In his hands, everything has a simple solution. He does not get lost in the details and you always leave with some encouragement."

But everyone understood that Archbishop Lefebvre arrived on the scene rather late to suppress some doctrinal, liturgical and disciplinary deviations, which had causes that were already ingrained. Nevertheless, he worked at it, and first at keeping the custom of wearing the cassock!

"Your Cassock Is a Sermon"

At the very start of his term as Superior General, on February 11, 1963, Archbishop Lefebvre sent a circular letter telling the Spiritans to keep wearing the cassock, contrary to the decision of the French bishops to accept "clerical garb," a decision that led to the toleration of lay clothing.

"Here is what I am going to write to our confreres," he announced to his secretary: "Your cassock is your religious habit, therefore you will keep it!"

"Oh, *Monseigneur*, they will tell you: 'The habit does not make the monk!'"

"On the contrary: the religious habit does much to inspire and to maintain the religious spirit; and so, as they say, 'You recognize the monk by his habit!'"

Aware of the importance of his decision and also of the power of the media, he had large excerpts from this letter published in the daily newspaper *Le Monde* and in the weekly *Rivarol*. "Lay clothing," he wrote, "the disappearance of all witness by the way he dresses, is on the priest's part a lack of faith in his priesthood, an underestimation of the religious sense of his neighbor and moreover an excess of cowardice, a lack of courage and of convictions. All this comes from a desire to align himself with the laicized, de-Christianized world. It is a mistake to think that the human soul is indifferent to spiritual things and to the desire for the things of heaven. By his cassock, the priest is a living sermon of the evangelical counsels of poverty and chastity, and of the virtue of penance. On the contrary, the absence of any apparent priest, especially in a large city, is a retreat in the preaching of the Gospel."

The publication of this text immediately won for Archbishop Lefebvre the deep satisfaction of many priests and lay Catholics who hate "priests in civilian clothing." "Who is this Lefebvre? Let us get acquainted with him!" But it also aroused the opposition and wrath of some of his brother priests and bishops. A sign of contradiction: that is what this disturbing Archbishop was becoming.

"Let Us Get Rid of the Professors Imbued with Modernism!"

Three years later, in 1965, just before the conclusion of Vatican Council II, which as we have seen promised *aggiornamento* or *The Church Suited to Today's Taste* [*L'Église mise au goût du jour*], as a book by Father Louis Coache was entitled, the Superior General had to denounce the disasters caused in the Congregation by the general spinelessness of authority that denies itself:

"The resignation of authority in practice causes subjects to abandon the imitation of Jesus Christ, and this abandonment leads to relaxation, a lack of modesty, a lack of self-respect and of respect for one's neighbor, which are contrary to self-mastery and to the order willed by God, and this leads to license and impurity. Let us make our *aggiornamento* not along the lines of a neo-Protestantism that destroys the sources of holiness, but rather inflamed by the holy desires that inspired the saints who were reformers, agents of renewal, because they loved Our Lord on the cross, practicing obedience, poverty and chastity; thus they acquired the spirit of sacrifice, offering, and prayer which transformed them into apostles."

Such cruel, inflammatory admonitions displeased the Spiritans who were won over to the idea of "openness to the world," which was the watchword of the craftsmen of the Council. Complaints against Archbishop Lefebvre arrived in Rome and reached the ears Pope Paul VI, who summoned the Superior: "*Monseigneur,* they tell me that 'Archbishop Lefebvre sins by authoritarianism, consults no one, governs according to his personal, outmoded views, imposes his ideas on the liturgical language and opposes the French episcopate.'"

"On the contrary, Holy Father," the Archbishop said to justify himself. "I multiply the meetings for consultation and exchange at all levels; I have two Assistants and four General Councilors and do not always do what I would like!"

"Would you like me to write a letter to the members of your Congregation telling them to obey you?"

"Oh, no, Holy Father. All that I ask is that you do not admit that these accusations have any validity. My confreres must not think that I came to ask you to support me."

Confronting the "Vocations Crisis"

And Archbishop Lefebvre got down to the real reforms. They were made necessary first by a change of mentality with regard to "vocations": The formerly flourishing minor seminaries, promising places where pious, studious adolescents could hear the call to the priesthood, were now deserted.

"Well, then, let's close them!" said Father Hirtz, the First General Councilor.

"No, not yet," the Archbishop replied, "but it is true that the time will come when our simple Catholic boys' boarding schools will play the role of minor seminaries, as my own college of Tourcoing did not long ago: in my day, in the graduating class, more than half of the students were headed for religious life or for the seminary!"

"Right, *Monseigneur*," said Father Hack, First Assistant, "but what steps are to be taken given the 'vocations crisis'? We have fewer and fewer young men entering our novitiates!"

"Let us speak about a crisis of families and of Catholic schools," Archbishop Lefebvre corrected him: "there lies the real need for renewal! This is what I did in Dakar and what I would have done in Tulle, and I would have had vocations, because ..."

Father Hirtz interrupted: "Then, too, the religious vows that we take frighten young people. They want to be missionaries, priests, yes, but not religious."

"And that is an error," said the Superior General.

"Explain that, *Monseigneur*, to our Spiritan confreres whose opinions tend toward that error, so that we might preach the opportune truth."

The Superior General composed a few lines in May 1967:

"A soul perfectly characterized by the gift of piety, which is given superabundantly in the priesthood and in the religious profession of the three vows, will thirst for religion, adoration, devotion, prayer, self-sacrifice, but also for union with God. Blessed is he who brings his intellect and his heart close to Christ Jesus during his novitiate! He will have increased his apostolic energies tenfold!"

But then came 1968 and the student revolt.

"Alas, *Monseigneur*," Father Hack announced, "I just learned that the novices in Gemert (Holland) have refused to take their vows!"

"We will be obliged to close our novitiates," Father Hirtz opined.

"I will resign myself to it, but so as to postpone the novitiate to the end of the two years of philosophy, for example," Archbishop Lefebvre proposed, "and to institute a preparatory year before sacred studies. Alas, our philosophy students are the ones who need a spiritual life most of all, even before their studies!"

A Spiritual Year, for Lack of a Novitiate

"But how can we initiate them to it now?" Father Hack asked.

"I have an idea about that.... Let me give it time to mature, and I will present it to you."

And indeed, one of his close collaborators, Father Antoine Nibel, testified:

"Archbishop Lefebvre is able to present his thought clearly, giving the impression of a grasp of concrete things, and also of an understanding of ready-made, well-ordered things in his mind, in the form of projects that are so various as to seem contradictory, but ready to execute as demanded by his sense of events and his ability to evaluate the opportunity that is to be taken."

The Superior General explained his innovative idea of a "novitiate without being one":

"A spiritual year that would not be a novitiate.... Do you know, sometimes I had the idea of reestablishing, as a second branch of the Congregation, the 'Gentlemen of the Holy Ghost' of Venerable Poullart des Places, our first founder: they did not take religious vows, but made simple commitments to the common life and to the practice of the priestly and religious virtues."

"Develop this idea in more depth, *Monseigneur*!"

Archbishop Lefebvre would develop it "in depth": it would be ready two years later, in 1970, but not for his Congregation.... For the moment, in other circular letters, the Archbishop insisted on the interior life, common prayers, regular community life, fleeing from the spirit of the world, parlors with windows in the houses in which to receive women or adolescent girls, and limited television viewing! It was quite late to reestablish order and the right spirit!

To his Irish confrere and friend, Father Michael O'Carroll, he confided: "It is impossible in practice to continue to direct a Congregation that does not listen to me, that wants no more to do with me!"

"But what will you do, *Monseigneur*?"

"Resign during the General Business Chapter, in September 1968; and you will see: I will found a traditional international seminary, and in ten years I will have a hundred seminarians!"

CHAPTER XIX

For the Catholic Priesthood 1962-1969

Ten years earlier, Archbishop Lefebvre did not yet have any idea about an international seminary. One Sunday in August of 1959 he was gladly attending the High Mass for the centenary of the death of the saintly Curé of Ars celebrated by one of his missionaries in the cathedral in Dakar and following attentively the rite of the Holy Sacrifice, the priest's gestures, the unbloody Immolation that they carried out. Kneeling on his prie-Dieu, he thought and he prayed:

"My God, in some of Your priests I sense impatience with the Church's tradition, contempt for the liturgical rites, the itch for novelty, the disappearance of piety, indifference toward sanctity. . . ."

Deep in his reflections, the Archbishop was absorbed in prayer and was then transported into a sort of dream. Perhaps he saw himself in a large church with many young clerics prostrated on the ground while he prepared to ordain them priests, to transmit to them the priesthood of Our Lord Jesus Christ.

"Yes," he dreamed, almost in spite of himself, "To confront the progressive degradation of the priestly ideal, transmit the Catholic priesthood of Our Lord Jesus Christ in all its doctrinal purity, in all its missionary charity, as it was transmitted to His Apostles and as the Roman Church transmitted it until the mid-twentieth century." And the dream became clearer by itself:

"Transmit not only the authentic Catholic priesthood, not only the sound doctrine approved by the Church, but also the profound and unchangeable spirit of the Catholic priesthood and of the

Christian spirit essentially connected with Our Lord's great prayer which eternally expresses His Sacrifice on the cross."

In other words, adoration, piety, renunciation, sacrifice, love of Tradition, the true charity of Jesus Christ.

When he emerged from this "dream" he wondered: "Where will this be? When will this be? Is it a premonition? I don't know. God is not obliged to tell us in advance what we must do. I just have to follow Divine Providence. God writes the main part, as in music, and I will have to write only the accompaniment, by trying not to play wrong notes!"

"My Son Wants to Be a Priest; Do Something for Him!"

Three years later, Archbishop Lefebvre, elected Superior of the Spiritans, as we saw, settled in the General House on rue Lhomond in Paris in August 1962. No sooner did he arrive than he was bombarded by requests from several families, whom he received kindly in his large, solemn office.

"*Monseigneur*, thank you for your letter of support to Jean Ousset and his Cité Catholique! *Monseigneur*, we have confidence in you: here is our son, who wants to become a priest but cannot find a seminary worthy of the name. Do something for him!"

"Do something," Marcel thought. "Could this be the hour of Divine Providence?"

"Dear sir, I am not yet free to do that, but I simply advise you to send your son to my dear old French Seminary in Rome, I hope that it has kept the sound doctrine and the correct traditions."

So it was that around twenty young Frenchmen entered Santa Chiara between 1962 and 1968. They often came to visit the Archbishop in the little apartment run by the Lithuanian Sisters on the via Casalmonferrato that he occupied in Rome. They confided in him:

"The rector no longer wants us to wear our cassocks; he does not let us pray the Rosary together in the chapel; and at the Gregorian University they have stopped offering courses in Latin...."

"Well, I will see.... Make sure you avoid public disputes. Each one of you should go and talk to the rector, pray, work and give good example. Study and meditate on your future priesthood in calm, recollection and discipline."

The Archbishop looked for alternative solutions for them. In 1968 he said to one of them, Jean-Yves Cottard, who described a revolutionary situation at the seminary: "I will find for you a bishop to ordain you...."

"*Monseigneur*, it is not a bishop that I want, it is you, *Monseigneur*!"

"You are not the first to ask me this, there are several of you. I will think about it. The University of Fribourg in Switzerland is rather good...."

"Just Do Something, *Monseigneur*!"

One fine day in June 1969, Professor Bernard Faÿ jumped for joy—despite his inflamed hip joint—in his elegant apartment on Grand'rue in Fribourg, overlooking the deep valley of the Sarine River and, on the other bank, the handsome convent of the Benedictines of Maigrauge. He had invited to his home Father Marie Dominique Philippe, a Dominican and a professor at the Catholic University of Fribourg, and Dom Bernard Kaul, Cistercian Abbot of Hauterive, as well as Archbishop Lefebvre, who agreed to come. There they were, all three, in his office, as well as two seminarians, two young men, Paul Aulagnier and Pierre Piqué, whom the Archbishop had sent to Santa Chiara; the seminary had just refused to admit the latter to Holy Orders....

Gesturing toward the two young men in cassocks, Bernard Faÿ exclaimed: "*Monseigneur*, do something for these seminarians!"

"Dear Professor, I sent them to Rome with twenty others, to my old seminary. But the seminary doesn't want them anymore. I have looked for solutions everywhere: Father Théodossios in Rome, the Abbey in Maylis, the Brothers of Saint Vincent de Paul in Érigné, Fontgombault Abbey."

"Ah, *Monseigneur*," Father Philippe exclaimed, "They must come to Fribourg! At the University they will support the professors who are still faithful to the teaching of Saint Thomas Aquinas."

"*Monseigneur*," the professor added, "you are free now, no longer burdened by the responsibility of being Superior of the Spiritans; isn't this Providential? Find a house in Fribourg."

"Do it, *Monseigneur*," exclaimed Father Philippe while effusively kissing the Archbishop's pastoral ring.

The Archbishop felt driven to make a serious decision: to commit himself to found something.

"But," he would say later, "I was sluggish and dragged my feet; I told myself: 'I will find them a priest to direct that house.' That was all!"

"Good!" he said to his interlocutors, "tomorrow I will go see Msgr. Charrière at the chancery; I am acquainted with him. If he gives me the green light, it will be the sign from Providence."

And the next day, on June 6, 1969, in the chancery in Fribourg:

"Well, this is early! *Monseigneur* Lefebvre! Come right in. Ah, I still remember you from Fatick!"

"Yes, I had invited you to consecrate that brand new church, built by the generous tithes of your Swiss Catholics: dear Doctor Schorer, the 'mendicant millionaire' of Fribourg, and that lady with the little Swiss knives …"

"Madame Elsener, from Victorinox!"

"Yes, she's the one."

"You played a trick on me then!"

"What do you mean?" Archbishop Lefebvre asked.

"Well, to start with: the church that you had me consecrate: it was a notorious ceremony that lasted a good four hours. Then the fifty baptisms that you had me administer! Fifty by me and fifty by you and another fifty by your Auxiliary Msgr. Guibert! That made three endless lines. A day for the record books! But to what do I owe your visit?"

"Your Excellency, I have here and there some young men who have started their clerical studies with the approval of their bishops, in order to become priests; they could benefit by taking the courses at the University of Fribourg. I would have to find a house...."

"Go right ahead, *Monseigneur*! I will not recommend my seminary, where there is hardly any discipline. I am pessimistic about the future of priestly formation here. So look for a house in Fribourg, I won't stop you at all!"

The Seminary Opens Its Doors

And so, on October 13, 1969, nine young men—including the two who were already wearing the cassock—appeared at 10 route de Marly, the "Don Bosco Home": seven Frenchmen, one Swiss from Jura and an Argentine sent by Father Michel André, a Spiritan missionary in Entrerrios. On that day, the anniversary of the miracle of the sun at Fatima, the Immaculate Virgin became involved in the enterprise. Now, when she intervenes, it is for the good!

But then right at the last minute the priest on whom Archbishop Lefebvre was counting to direct the little community let him down: he didn't show! Thus Divine Providence willed that Msgr. Lefebvre personally assume all the responsibility in an adventure that he glimpsed while remembering his "dream in Dakar." Immediately the prelate, an Archbishop, former Apostolic Delegate of Pius XII, set about explaining to the nine untutored neophytes the rudiments of spiritual doctrine and the principles of the rule of life that he himself composed for his "international Seminary of Saint Pius X": rise at 5:30 a.m., meditation, Holy Mass ... and at 7:00 p.m. the Rosary recited for the benefactors, meals taken in common, common evening prayer—and no television! "The tabernacle is our true television, which puts us in contact with the heavenly realities!"

CHAPTER XX

The Priestly Society
of Saint Pius X
1970

So here was Archbishop Lefebvre, director of this *"Convict Saint-Pie-X,"* a seminary without the name, at the head of nine young men who were truly seminarians, because three days later, to their great joy, he clothed them with the cassock. All this is done, he claimed, "in spite of him"; but not without him!

An Idea of the Future

But what was this that he was proposing to them already on November 15, 1969, one month after their entrance?

"What will you become after your ordination? Will you disperse to your home dioceses, isolated, exposed to the influence of a clergy with Modernist tendencies? Would it not be better to stay together?"

"How would we do that?" Paul Aulagnier asked.

"By forming a 'Priestly Society.' It would be a society of common life without vows, but with commitments. The common life of the clergy is quite traditional in the Church; it promotes fidelity, a life of study and union with God, the practice of fraternal charity, an organized apostolate. And the primary aims of this institute would be priestly formation in seminaries and the sanctification of priests."

"*Monseigneur,*" said Father Paul, "the future will no doubt prove you right!"

"I will place this Society under the patronage of Saint Pius X, whose motto will be ours: 'To restore all things in Christ.'"

At the following recreation, young Bernard Tissier de Mallerais asked his older fellow seminarian Paul Aulagnier: "Even so, it is a bit mysterious. When could *Monseigneur* have started to think about this 'Society'?"

"The visit paid us recently by Father Boissard of Lendreville, who gathers priests who unfortunately have been unfaithful to their vocation and has them do manual work to instill in them again the love of their priesthood, reminds me of the 'Priestly Fraternity' founded by Father Eugène Prévost for the sanctification of priests who are elderly, sick or unfaithful to their priesthood, but to tell the truth, not to run seminaries. But even so, 'Priestly Society'!"

"*Monseigneur* must have been thinking for a long time about this 'Society' that he explained to us, or else God is the one who has been thinking about it for him for a very long time!"

"We Are Keeping the Old Mass!"

On the eve of the First Sunday of Advent in 1969, November 30, when a beastly cold had already frozen Fribourg, *Monseigneur* spoke seriously to them:

"Tomorrow, here in Fribourg and throughout the world, a new Mass will be imposed.... You know that I have had it examined by Roman theologians; the result was a *Short Critical Study* signed by two Cardinals, Bacci and Ottaviani, and forwarded to Pope Paul VI. It reads:

"'The *Novus Ordo* represents, both as a whole and in its details, a striking departure from the Catholic theology of the Mass as it was formulated in Session XXII of the Council of Trent. The «canons» of the rite definitively fixed at that time provided an insurmountable barrier to any heresy directed against the integrity of the Mystery.'"

He explained: "This new Mass departs from the doctrine of the Council of Trent. First by the definition of it that Paul VI gives in the *Institutio generalis*: a 'synaxis presided by the priest,' and by its content, it blurs three truths of the faith: the Real Presence of Christ and the transubstantiation that carries it out; the propitiatory sacrifice that is offered in it; the offering thereof by the priest alone in the person of Christ."

And he added: "Pope Paul VI did not take into account some very serious reasons mentioned by these Cardinals. But Rome does not insist on the application of the *Novus Ordo* before November 1971, and therefore ..."

Then he posed the question to his seminarians: "What will we do?"

In his soft voice he questioned as though he did not know what to do. But he knew very well. A short silence ensued.

One of the seminarians, Bernard Pellabeuf, thought: "Well, I did not come here to follow the liturgical reform, which is already suppressing Latin and turning the altars around!"

Georges Monti thought: "I've had enough of the chatter that prevents recollection; it has been going on since 1965."

Paul Aulagnier mused: "And now it's a revolution; its author, Father Bugnini, said: 'This is a new creation.'"

Maxime Doyon pondered: "And those six Protestant pastors whom Paul VI invited to give their advice in this mess!"

Then *Monseigneur* broke in: as though timid, he asks again in his soft little voice: "Don't you think? We will keep the Old Mass!"

History will tell what heroism was concealed in that little sentence, with what impact it would demolish the whole conciliar edifice, what strength it would give to the Church, to the Church of all ages!

Trial and Temptation Overcome

But did God bless the founder's decision right away?

He fell ill and asked for Extreme Unction; four seminarians influenced by Solesmes—"It is necessary to obey"—left him; an interim rector told those who remain: "You can skip the cassock to go to classes at the University."

Then the Archbishop himself, having just recovered from his illness, was shaken: "My dear friends, the experiment does not seem to be a success. I will place you in the Salesianum, a boarding house for ecclesiastical students, and I will find a bishop to ordain you...."

"*Monseigneur*," said Father Paul, "We will not leave you!"

"These are the seminarians," the Archbishop acknowledged, "who by their reactions have pointed out to me the path of Divine Providence."

The Statutes of the Priestly Society of Saint Pius X

Then, calm again and determined, the Archbishop got down to the work of composing the statutes for the "Priestly Society of Saint Pius X." "It is centered on the celebration of the Holy Sacrifice of the Mass, the proclamation of the Kingship of Christ the Priest, since Jesus reigns through the wood of His cross; it is dedicated first to the formation of holy Catholic priests and then to the priestly apostolate and to everything that promotes the priesthood or follows from it."

The virtues of its members would be:

"A great love for God, the Holy Trinity, which gives rise to chastity and poverty, and urges them to dedicate themselves through faith and prompt, generous and loving obedience. This charity will arouse in them thirst for the virtue of justice, in other words, first for the dispositions of devotion, adoration and prayer which will help them to carry out with the utmost perfection the most sublime act of Christian prayer: the Holy Sacrifice of the Mass; with an ardent devotion to the Eucharist and the Virgin Mary in her Compassion with Jesus, the Priest and Victim for the redemption of our sins. The habit of the members, expressing their detachment from the world, will be the cassock, which is at the same time a witness and a sermon: it drives away the evil spirits and attracts upright minds and religious souls. It greatly facilitates the apostolate...."

The Approval of Bishop Charrière

Throughout the summer of 1970, Bishop Charrière, who received the draft of the statutes, vacillated. His Auxiliary Bishop, Msgr. Mamie, warned him: "Don't approve this 'Society'; it is not in the spirit of the Council!"

By dint of his insistent telephone calls, the Archbishop was received at the chancery on November 8, 1970.

"I have your document," Bishop Charrière told him. "I am having it typed by my secretary. Wait in the chapel!"

And after fervent prayer, when Archbishop Lefebvre emerged from the oratory: "Here are your statutes, *Monseigneur*, duly approved! And your Priestly Society is explicitly erected in this diocese as a 'pious union'—the first step toward erection as a society of diocesan right—for six years, renewable by tacit agreement."

Back at the house in Vignettaz, where the seminarians were waiting for him, *Monseigneur*, radiant, showed the decree, the seal and the Bishop's signature: "This is our birth certificate! Dated All Saints Day. On that day the Church is approving this little work to safeguard the Catholic priesthood. We exist canonically. Without the erection of the Society by the local ordinary, I could not act for this cause. It had to be of the Church."

Domestic Church: Lefebvre Family

1909. Marcel aged four.

Vocation

1919. Marcel in the Eucharistic Crusade.

The Big Decision

1921: Marcel at Sacred Heart College [high school].

Roman Seminarian

1923-30. Marcel and seminarians at the French Seminary.

A Momentous Corpus Christi

1931. Curate at Lomme, France. The Archbishop is pictured here with the parish Catholic Action group.

At the Seminary in Libreville

1934. Professor at the seminary in Libreville, Gabon

On the Banks of the Ogooué

The Ogooué, the principal river of Gabon, is 750 miles long and navigable from Ndjole [Gabon] to the sea.

His Battle of Mortain

From 1945-47, Fr. Lefebvre was superior of the
Scholasticate of Philosophy in Mortain, France.

Archbishop of Dakar

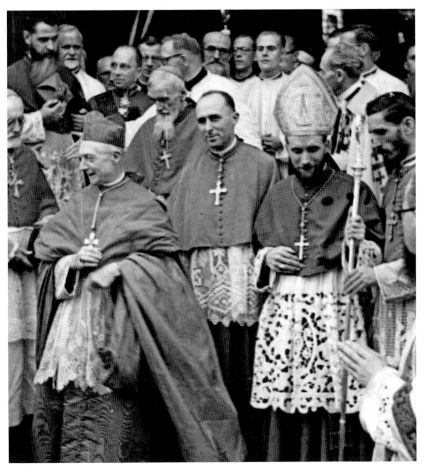

On December 18, 1947, Cardinal Achille Liénart, the Bishop of Lille, consecrated Marcel Lefebvre in the Church of Notre Dame des Anges in Tourcoing, France.

Apostolic Delegate

September 22, 1948. Archbishop Lefebvre is appointed
Apostolic Delegate to West Africa.

Infamous Inter-Religious Ceremony

Our Lady of Victories cathedral in Dakar.

New Laborers for the Gospel

During the 1950's religious from around the world were recruited by Archbishop Lefebvre to assist in the African missions.

Pope John XXIII

May 7, 1962. Archbishop Lefebvre is granted an audience with Pope John XXIII.

Hope for a Diocese in Danger

1962. Appointed bishop of Tulle, a poor diocese in central France.

Confronting the Conciliar Deviations

In 1960 Archbishop Lefebvre was appointed to the
Central Preparatory Commission for Vatican Council II.

Opposing Liberalism

1963. The *Coetus Internationalis Patrum* was founded to provide an effective opposition to the liberal domination of the Council.

The Battles at the Council

Archbishop Lefebvre with leading members of the *Coetus*.
Bishop de Castro Mayer can be seen third from the right.

Superior General of the Spiritans

On July 26, 1962, the Chapter General of the
Congregation of the Holy Spirit elected Archbishop
Lefebvre as Superior General.

For the Catholic Priesthood

Archbishop Lefebvre visits the seminary in Argentina.

The Priestly Society of Saint Pius X

October 13, 1969. Archbishop Lefebvre opens the
"International House of St. Pius X" in Fribourg.

The Seminary in Ecône

October 1, 1970. The Archbishop opens a "year of spirituality" at Ecône in Valais, Switzerland.

The New Mass

". . . I say that this new Mass is bad in itself, in its rite and not only in the manner of celebrating it [. . .] but precisely because this rite no longer clearly expresses a sacrifice offered by Jesus Christ to God His Father, in propitiation for the offense given to God by our sins . . ."

The Condemnation

May 6, 1975. The Holy See "authorized" Bishop Mamie of Fribourg to "withdraw the approval" given to the Society of Saint Pius X by his predecessor Bishop Charrière.

"The Hot Summer" of 1976

August 29, 1976. Archbishop Lefebvre celebrated a public Mass in the sports stadium of the trade fair in Lille, with a crowd of 7,000 Catholics and the media in attendance.

The Council in Light of Tradition

"We can make the well-founded statement, by arguments both of external criticism and of internal criticism, that the spirit which dominated the Council and inspired so many of its ambiguous and even frankly erroneous texts was not that of the Holy Ghost" (*I Accuse the Council!*).

Sisters, Brothers and Schools

1982. Archbishop Lefebvre with SSPX Sisters and students of St. Mary's Academy, St. Marys, Kansas.

The Archbishop in America

1977-84. Archbishop Lefebvre visiting St. Marys.

Toward The Consecrations

". . . without a faithful bishop, believers will be deprived of the faithful and assuredly valid priesthood."

Roman Negotiation

May 5, 1988: Signing the "Protocol." Frs. Laroche and Tissier de Mallerais (standing) were the Society's negotiators.

A Magnanimous Act

1988. Preaching the sermon at the Episcopal
Consecrations in Ecône.

Charity of a Pastor

Archbishop Lefebvre at St. Nicholas du Chardonnet, Paris.

Strength and Gentleness

"Our Lord is the only man who is God! Therefore He is King. Therefore He must reign, consequently he has something to say about everything."

The Founder and His Seminarians

"What a job! What work you will have to accomplish, my dear friends! You are the 'little remnant' which nevertheless boldly carries the torch."

Archbishop Lefebvre Up Close

Archbishop Lefebvre in his office at the seminary in Ecône.

A Priest of the Church

Archbishop Lefebvre performs a baptism in the seminary chapel at Ecône.

Heavenly Reward

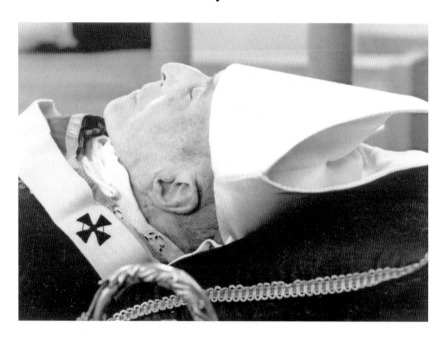

CHAPTER XXI

The Seminary in Ecône

"Come on, Alphonse, drink a round with us. Have you heard the news? Ecône is for sale! The canons of the Grand Saint-Bernard are selling the house and its vineyards. There's talk of making it into a bawdy house. . . ."

It was Holy Thursday in the year 1968. Alphonse Pedroni left the Saxon Café distressed and met his friend Gratien Rausis: "Gratien, we have to prevent that! They are quite capable of blowing up the chapel!"

"Let's buy it. But with what?"

The banker inquired. "Six hundred thousand francs!? Do you have funds of your own to secure the loan?"

"No," said Marcel, Alphonse's brother, "we have nothing! This is for a religious work. Lend us the money anyway!"

The banker, wide-eyed, gives in. Ecône is rescued. The two Pedroni brothers and Gratien were joined by Roger Lovey, a lawyer, and Guy Genoud, a politician.

In the Chapel of Our Lady of the Fields, the five friends from Valais, Switzerland, together with Father Epiney, the young curate of Riddes, sung a *Salve Regina* in thanksgiving on May 31, 1968. This deserted chapel was calling priests and, who knows, future priests. . . .

The Paths of Providence

A year passes and there was Archbishop Lefebvre in Valais, as if by chance; for God, though, nothing happens by chance! The

Archbishop preached the First Holy Communion retreat in Fully, at the parish of his friend from Santa Chiara, Father Henri Bonvin.

"By the way, *Monseigneur*, are you looking for a house for future priests? I might have what you need...."

The next day, during morning Mass, while distributing Communion, the curate, ciborium in hand, whispered to his parishioner Roger Lovey: "Roger, come see me in the sacristy!"

And there he said, "I have Archbishop Lefebvre visiting, who is looking for a house for future priests. Would Ecône be available?"

And the next day, at the rectory:

"Yes," *Monseigneur* explained, "for future seminarians, to whom I am thinking of offering a year of spiritual preparation, a sort of novitiate for future priests so that they can learn to know Our Lord Jesus Christ intimately."

In late April in 1969, that oasis of apricot trees in bloom, and that still arid vineyard which a solid dike protects from the incursions of a gushing cascade, seemed to the Archbishop to be the ideal remote corner, with the old house of the canons, its walls made of roughly squared rocks, a shale roof and corridors paved with large slabs of shale: "Now that's solid!" the visitor said to himself.

Another year passed.

Finally in April 1970, having tonsured Paul Aulagnier and ordained Pierre Piqué to the subdiaconate, in the shrine in Bourguillon dedicated to Our Lady Guardian of the Faith, and at the conclusion of a walk to the Carthusian house in Valsainte, Archbishop Lefebvre once again met the attorney, Lovey, who told him: "*Monseigneur*, Ecône is still available!"

"Thank you, Sir. Then I will have to meet *Monseigneur* Adam, Bishop of Sion; I need his permission."

During his meeting at the chancery in Sion, he went about his business with boldness and discretion; it was a diplomatic master stroke:

"*Monseigneur*, would you agree to accept into your seminary for the Diocese of Sion four aspirants to the priesthood whom I am looking after?"

"Well, I just transferred my seminary close to Fribourg so that my seminarians can take courses at the University! No, really, that will not work, I'm sorry."

"Then, *Monseigneur*, do you authorize me at least to place next year other future candidates for clerical studies in a house in Valais, in Ecône, which Attorney Roger Lovey would be willing to place at my disposal? It would be a preparatory year before they begin to study philosophy and theology."

The Bishop of Sion did not dare refuse the second request of his enterprising colleague. "Fine! For your 'preparatory year' no objection, *Monseigneur*. But for a seminary, I have difficulty seeing it in Valais, where we have the scholasticates of the Capuchins, the Canons of Saint Bernard and the Canons of Saint Maurice."

Bishop Adam's Agreement

Archbishop Lefebvre thanked Nestor Adam but had a strong sense of the latter's reluctance concerning a whole seminary in Valais. That was when he had a moment of discouragement, as we related earlier. But he overcame it quickly: twelve candidates applied for the following academic year. Several of them came from the circles of Cité Catholique and the Knights of Our Lady, dynamic young men who were well trained for doctrinal combat. Another, a former non-commissioned officer in Indochina, won a medal for his military service, and a former Cistercian novice, Bernard Waltz, was competent in all questions about organizing personnel and materiel.

Just at that moment three young priests, Jacques Masson, Maurice Gottlieb and Claude Michel, were providentially free and willing to supervise the young recruits: they would teach in Ecône the courses on spirituality, liturgy, Latin and Gregorian chant.

And for the four "seniors" who would continue their course-work at the University of Fribourg, the Archbishop bought a quaint villa on rue de la Vignettaz in Fribourg. He furnished it, found a cook and settled his four philosophy students there; they were joined by Bernard Waltz and Jean-Yves Cottard, theologians. This was in October 1970.

Now in the first months of 1971, troubles broke out at the University; there were student protests against some excellent professors. Then in Ecône the professors talked among themselves and proposed to Archbishop Lefebvre: "Why not set up the whole seminary in Ecône?"

"Yes, I'm thinking of doing that," the prelate replied. "I want these young men to have the benefit of receiving true, simple teaching, of being in a setting that is peaceful, not contentious, of being in the midst of nature, in this province of Valais which is still profoundly faithful."

Cardinal Journet, when consulted in Geneva, was deliberately evasive but seemed to support the idea: "The University is not for everyone.... If you have academically gifted candidates, yes, send them to the University."

Bishop Mamie himself was in favor: the seminary would not be in his diocese.... All that remains was to get authorization from Msgr. Nestor Adam. It looked like it will be an uphill battle. "Ecône?" Nestor objected. "Is that a good choice of location? The religious of Saint Bernard housed their young theologians there for several years under Canon Berthod, and they have left. And where will you find professors in that out-of-the-way place?"

"I already have the three whom you have met, and I have several others in mind."

Then, worn out by the persistent requests, Nestor gave in: "It is true that the Capuchins have closed their scholasticate.... Well, *Monseigneur*, I have no objection!"

But when Archbishop Lefebvre asks him for written authorization, Nestor, smiling faintly, replied: "You doubt the word of a bishop?"

Archbishop Lefebvre would have nothing written. That way Nestor Adam would be able to say: "That was done without my authorization." Half-truth, half-lie.

On the basis of this half-spoken permission, the Archbishop launched into the construction of three new buildings at Ecône, spread out over several years: first, a residential building.

Construction Projects in Ecône

The architect Ami Delaloye had just presented the plans in Ecône on February 15, 1971, and their price tag: one million five hundred thousand Swiss francs. The Archbishop listened but thought: "I need one third of that sum in order to begin without having to borrow. I don't have it, and therefore I'm not going ahead...."

At that very moment the telephone rang in the next room. Mademoiselle Mauvais, the receptionist, opened the door partially: "*Monseigneur*, a telephone call for you!"

"I'm coming!"

On the other end of the line: "Hello, *Monseigneur*, Brother Christian here, from the Spiritan bursar's office in Fribourg. *Monseigneur*, someone has just deposited in your account the sum of 600,000 francs; he will write to you."

The donor in question was Bishop Adrien Bressolles, a prelate friend, former Chaplain General of the French Navy and President of the Pontifical Missionary Work of the Holy Childhood in France.

The Archbishop went back to his meeting. "We will begin," he said simply.

On April 28 the architect returned; he had finalized the work program, he had chosen local businesses; several of the bosses would become friends of Ecône. *Monseigneur* was assisted by his

Spiritan confrere, Father Berclaz, a construction specialist, who testified: "I truly admire the spiritual approach, the spirituality that he managed to put into this construction site. He started with a prayer, and quite a few of the contractors present were coming more or less for free."

The Curriculum at the Seminary

Elsewhere, the plan of studies was quickly sketched, reduced to the minimum because of the immediate need for young priests.

Besides the spirituality year, there would be two years of philosophy according to Saint Thomas, "with a manual," *Monseigneur* proposed.

"Hmm," says Father Thomas d'Aquin, "you know, *Monseigneur*, I would prefer the properly philosophical method of discovering principles starting from common sense applied to natural realities."

"Okay! But Sacred Scripture and apologetics will be taught during these years of philosophy along with the beginnings of moral theology. This spiritual component will prevent our philosophers from becoming arid. Then two years of theology will follow: dogma with the *Summa* of Saint Thomas and moral theology...."

"With the textbook by Father Prümmer, O.P.," Canon Berthod suggested. Forced to leave the priory in Lens (Valais), he would become one of the professors.

"And," *Monseigneur* added, "something new but traditional: as I had it fifty years ago in Santa Chiara, during the spirituality year there will be a special course on the 'Documents of the Magisterium' about the modern errors denounced by the popes, and the seminarians will be encouraged to read anti-liberal Catholic authors: Cardinal Pie, Louis Veuillot (*The Liberal Illusion*), Cardinal Billot, and more recent writers: Léon de Poncins, Jean Ousset (*That He May Reign*)."

A Motley Faculty

The faculty members agreed with the Thomistic, militant views of the founder. They included, after all, a Canon of Saint Bernard, a fine humorist and a resolutely objective moralist: dear Canon René Berthod; a Belgian Oblate of Mary Immaculate and a gentle philosopher; a Benedictine from La Pierre-qui-Vire, a librarian (every day they feared that they would find him dead, crushed by the collapse of his bookshelves); a Discalced Carmelite, a scrupulous apologist, a priest from the Diocese of Bourges, a deaf historian with a delicious sense of humor; a father of a family, a former Protestant pastor who had become a priest; then two Dominican friars from Fribourg: Father Ceslas Spicq, a learned exegete, on points that are a bit modernist, and Father Thomas Mehrle, who skewered Karl Rahner and instilled a taste for Saint Thomas; and to top off this rather motley crew, dear Professor Faÿ who would reveal "the secret of the Freemasons" and of the esoteric sects, while Professor Gabriel Chabot, blind but clear-sighted when it comes to Christ the King, would come from Lausanne with his white cane to teach the beginners "*rosa*, a rose" [*i.e.* Latin].

Last but not least, one fine day in October 1971, Father Ludovic Marie Barrielle arrived in Ecône; he was a member of the Parish Cooperators of Christ the King, and *Monseigneur* had been acquainted with him since his days in Dakar. The fiery Catalan Father Francisco de Paula y Vallet, was the founder of that humble congregation dedicated to the preaching of the "Spiritual Exercises" of Saint Ignatius in five days. His right-hand man in France, Father Barrielle, former curate of Good Shepherd parish in Marseilles, a veteran of 1918, a former military chaplain in 1944, was an enthusiastic French Southerner; his Marseilles accent added warmth to his very sprightly language!

"*Monseigneur*," he said frankly, "my congregation is becoming Modernist. I have come to look for recruits to re-found our Cooperators within the orbit of Tradition."

"Oh, dear! Forget that, dear Father," *Monseigneur* Lefebvre replied. "Stay here and you will give spiritual conferences! You will provide 'the milk of the novices' and you can initiate the seminarians into the art of preaching Ignatian retreats."

"Divine Providence!" exclaimed the seminarian Philibert, "From now on the *Exercises*, a specialty of the Jesuits, will be preached by us, simple priests of the Society, to everyone, priests or laymen!"

And there you had Ecône, the "seminary of hope," in the heroic years 1970-1974, a rather uncommon seminary, and what a seminary rector! A bishop, "God's pirate, who scoured the ecclesiastical oceans to assemble a motley crew of professors," as Father Calmel memorably declared. Ecône soon sent its pioneers to England: to Southwark (London); to the United States: to San José, California, to New York and to Detroit, Michigan, where the first seminary of the Society in America was established; and in France, Le Pointet and Suresnes were the first two priories.

"I said to myself," the founder told his sons, "that the day when the Society becomes international, crossing the oceans, then I will know that this work is truly willed by God!"

The Problem of Attending the New Mass

On November 29, 1969, Archbishop Lefebvre therefore decided to "keep the Old Mass."

But since he was often absent in 1970 and 1971, he left his seminarians without a Mass. During the week, good Father Rivière, C.P.C.R., came from Grolley to the Don Bosco Home to celebrate the Holy Sacrifice. But on Sundays?

Which "Mass in Latin"?

"Why don't we go to the Benedictine monastery in Maigrauge?" Paul Aulagnier suggested. "An old Benedictine priest provides the Mass in Latin there."

"But it is the Mass of Paul VI in Latin," Ernesto Eraso objected.

"I will contact *Monseigneur!*" Later he told the founder: "*Monseigneur*, this Mass is celebrated reverently, the Offertory and the Canon are prayed silently, and what's more the sisters sing everything in Gregorian chant."

"Well, because it is the only option, I have no objection!"

But December approached.

"*Monseigneur*," Bernard Tissier asked, "where will we attend Mass during the Christmas vacation, especially on Sunday? With our families?"

"Look for a priest who keeps the Traditional Mass. And if you don't have one nearby, find a priest who keeps the Offertory of all ages: 'Receive, Holy Father, this spotless Victim ...' This prayer and the gestures of the one offering it ritually signify the sacrifice of the cross and thus strengthen the new rite, which is so meager: 'We offer this bread, fruit of the earth and work of human hands ...'"

"And if Catholics ask us, 'Can we attend the new Mass?', can we give them this advice: '[there has to be] at least the traditional Offertory'?"

"That is a more delicate question; if they do not even find that, I cannot deprive most Catholics of Sunday Mass; moreover, I don't have the authority to do so."

Intervention by Father Calmel

But as time went on, since the new rite more and more often manifested a contempt for the faith and for piety, being "sometimes scandalous or even sacrilegious," in the judgment of Archbishop Lefebvre, the founder would take a stronger position in practice. The retreat preached in Ecône by Father Calmel, O.P., was germane to the hardening of the Archbishop's directives. Here is what the preacher said to the seminarians on April 7, 1974:

"The Traditional Catholic, Gregorian Mass belongs to the Church, the new Mass belongs only to Modernism. I will therefore be a witness to the Mass; I will not tamper with the rites. Be able to abstain from Mass, so as not to give your backing as future priests to the new Modernist Mass. Let us testify by our stance that the Mass belongs to the Church and not to Modernism. A testimony is absolute. If I give testimony to the Catholic Mass, I must abstain from the others! It is like the pinch of incense offered to the idols! It is all or nothing! The moment you loosen something, you start misunderstandings. We must therefore be truly inflexible about our testimony concerning the Mass."

Some seminarians were surprised and frightened by these incisive remarks: "Really, Father is exaggerating!"

Others were enthusiastic about them. "Here is a true Dominican Father, *in quo non est dolus*, in whom there is no guile!"

Father Calmel described the spirit that should move everyone: "Such witness is possible only if we are prayerful souls, and if we give this witness with great charity, so as not to 'crack' under pressure. For the hard-hearted are the ones who crack. Our position is tenable only if we have a martyr's soul. The Fathers of the Church gave inflexible witness. What good would Saint Hilary have done if he had remained in Poitiers? If he had collaborated with Arianism? But no! Precisely because he was exiled to the farthest reaches of Asia Minor, which was no fun, he was useful to the Church! So it is no fun, but the love of God is what demands this of us, such an exhausting witness, with all the false problems of authority and obedience. The battle of faith is to maintain the faithful rite. To be confessors of the faith to our era is a great honor that God gives us. Whatever we may feel about being treated as disobedient, rebels, about being rejected, victims of 'sociological exile,' let us hold fast!"

And Father Calmel concluded with this motto, which was quite characteristic of his style: "Do not drag Saint Pius X to the Masses of the new religion!"

Archbishop Lefebvre Decides: "Stop Attending the New Mass!"

Then in 1975-1976, reinvigorated by the language of the uncompromising Dominican, Archbishop Lefebvre strengthened his position; he willingly explained it when answering the questions that people asked him.

"*Monseigneur*, do you say that this new Mass is invalid?"

"No, I don't say that it is invalid—although it often is, because the 'role of signification' is lacking in the new rite to express a propitiatory sacrifice, and hence it does not prevent a possible contrary intention on the part of the celebrant who would deliberately intend something else: such as a fraternal meal, or a sacred synaxis as the *Institutio generalis* of the *Novus Ordo Missae* says, or else a renewal of the Last Supper (Calvin), or even a simple commemoration of the sacrifice of the cross: 'It is simply a matter of remembering,' as the 1972 missal of the Bishops of France says."

"Well, then, *Monseigneur*, do you think that this new Mass is heretical?"

"I don't say either that this Mass is heretical or that it contains heresies, because in fact we find none in the rite; but it omits or diminishes the expression of the Catholic faith in a tendentious, Protestant way; this is why in one conference I called it 'Luther's Mass.' Six Protestant pastors were invited by Paul VI to give their opinions as the *Novus Ordo Missae* was being finalized."

"*Monseigneur*, is this Mass still Catholic, then?"

"I do not dare to say that it is not Catholic, but I describe its rite as a 'bastard rite,' that's a bit intense, but that's what it is: the rite is ambiguous. A priest can celebrate it with a Catholic intention, and a Protestant pastor can do so with his Protestant intention, as one of them said in 1970."

"Do you say at least that this Mass is bad?"

"Yes, I say that this new Mass is bad in itself, in its rite and not only in the manner of celebrating it or because of the scandalous abuses, but precisely because this rite no longer clearly expresses a sacrifice offered by Jesus Christ to God His Father, in propitiation for the offense given to God by our sins. It causes a loss of faith in the atoning sacrifice of the altar; I really must state that it is therefore dangerous to the faith; it is poisoned."

"If that is the case, can we attend it?"

"That is the practical application of what we just said: and first of all this Mass cannot be the object of the Sunday obligation: the Church cannot oblige us to take part in an ambiguous Mass."

"Next I come to the directive that I now give to faithful Catholics: Don't go to the new Mass. And on Sunday, if it is not possible for you to attend the Traditional Mass, stay at home, read and meditate on the texts of the Ordinary of the Mass, and also those of the 'proper' of the day; pray the Rosary and in that way sanctify the Lord's day. You can, however, be present at a new Mass, attending passively, on the occasion of the funeral of a friend or relative."

"*Monseigneur*," said Father Lancien, "that is not the position of Father Noël Barbara in his journal *Fortes in Fide* [Strong in Faith]! He demonstrates that the new Mass is invalid in itself!"

Father Sicaire asked, "Haven't others taken an exaggerated position by maintaining that this Mass is 'intrinsically bad' to the point where attending it would always be a sin?"

"More than one of our friends lacks balance," Archbishop Lefebvre dared to say. "I must often reassert the position that I consider the most theological and the most pastoral."

And indeed it must be noted that this well-pondered attitude "paid off": it was precisely what won for Archbishop Lefebvre the confidence of many faithful Catholics and what caused his success, we could say.

CHAPTER XXII

The Condemnation 1975

The bishops of France were on high alert. What was the matter? A heresy? A schism? A scandal caused by some wayward priests? Indeed, they sent Archbishop Etchegaray, Secretary of the Permanent Committee of the French Episcopal Conference, to the Secretary of State of Paul VI in Rome, French Cardinal Jean Villot.

"Your Eminence," said Etchegaray, "this cannot go on! This Lefebvre is taking all our vocations: they are going off to Ecône! Look, at the start of the academic year in 1973, Ecône already had ninety-three seminarians, most of them French!"

An Apostolic Visit to Ecône

Villot replied, "I will speak about this to the Holy Father, and he will order a canonical visit to this 'wildcat seminary,' as you call it: What Mass do they have? Do they follow the Council?"

And on November 11, 1974, two Apostolic Visitors, a bishop and a prelate, appeared in Ecône. They had to question the seminarians one by one.

"In your view," Bishop Onclin asked one of them, "is the Resurrection of Christ a physical resurrection? Is it an historical event?"

"Yes! Jesus was dead, then He is alive, therefore He rose, in his flesh and bones, early on Easter morning!"

"Oh, it's not so clear as that!"

Young Father du Chalard reported this exchange to Archbishop Lefebvre, who was scandalized by it. He set out for Rome to complain, but upon arriving in Rome he changed his mind: from his little Roman flat he composed in one sitting a declaration, a "position statement," which he would then read to the seminarians in Ecône.

The Statement Dated November 21, 1974

"We adhere with our whole heart, and with our whole soul to Catholic Rome, the Guardian of the Catholic Faith and of those traditions necessary for the maintenance of that Faith, to eternal Rome, Mistress of Wisdom and Truth. Because of this adherence we refuse and have always refused to follow the Rome of the neo-Modernist and neo-Protestant tendencies, such as were clearly manifested during the Second Vatican Council, and after the Council in all the resulting reforms ... which come from heresy and lead to heresy. The only attitude of fidelity to the Church, for our salvation, is the categorical refusal to accept these reforms...."

All the seminarians applauded—except Bernard Tissier de Mallerais: not that he disapproved of this text, its correctness and clarity, but he thought: "This declaration will be our condemnation!"

It was true: contrary to all human prudence, Archbishop Lefebvre was openly speaking his mind, in extremely strong, provocative terms: it was an inadvertent declaration of war.

But his observation that there are "two Romes": a Catholic Rome and a neo-Modernist Rome, agreed with the one made by Father Thomas Calmel, O. P., in an article published in the March 1967 issue of *Itinéraires* when he spoke about "the pseudo-Church of neo-Modernism."

Soon Archbishop Lefebvre was "invited" to a "conversation" in Rome; in fact he appeared before a commission of three cardinals appointed by Paul VI: Wright, former Bishop of Pittsburgh in the United States, Prefect of the Clergy in Rome; Garrone, an alumnus of Santa Chiara and Prefect of Seminaries, and Tabera, Prefect of Religious.

"Your manifesto is unacceptable," Garrone declared. "You say that 'no authority, not even the highest, can force us to abandon or to diminish our faith': even the highest! So even the Pope?"

"Yes, Your Eminence: if he promotes heresy like Pope Liberius in the fourth century, we can resist him as Saint Athanasius did!"

"And so you make yourself out to be Athanasius! You are mad, *Monseigneur!*"

"Thank you, Your Eminence."

The So-Called Suppression of the Society

And since the Archbishop did not retract his "manifesto," the Holy See "authorized" Bishop Mamie of Fribourg to "withdraw the approval" given to the Society of Saint Pius X by his predecessor Bishop Charrière; which Bishop Mamie did on May 6, 1975. The Society no longer had a canonical status!

"Should I submit?" the founder asked himself, "put the key under the mat, send my seminarians home, close our priories, have our priests return to their original dioceses, and should I make a docile retreat ... as Pope Paul VI already suggested to me? But letting everything go is not my style!"

He explained to his seminarians: "With a little sense of reality, with a true historical sense, we understand that this 'suppression' is just one episode in this gigantic struggle between the Church and the Revolution. With all that we represent: Latin, the true Holy Sacrifice, the authentic priesthood, Saint Thomas Aquinas, the traditional catechism, the faith of all ages—giving in would be doing the work of those who are demolishing the Church!"

He reacted also with this Letter to his Friends and Benefactors, which he read at the seminary:

"This suppression of the Society is unjust and invalid. I do not want to collaborate in the destruction of the Church by closing this seminary! When the Good Lord calls me home, I do not want to have to accuse myself: 'Well, I destroyed something that God had permitted me to do by His Providence.'"

Gentle Father de la Presle came to his office to object: "But you do have to obey the Pope."

"Dear Father, you know very well that Pope Paul VI admitted, in a speech, that we are experiencing 'the self-destruction of the Church'; well, then, I will not cooperate in that self-destruction, not that!"

"But couldn't you appeal to the Pope?"

"That is what I did: a canonical recourse to the tribunal of the Apostolic Signatura: to find out first whether the cardinalatial commission was formed by Paul VI, and then whether Paul VI approved its decision *in forma specifica*."

"And what response did the Apostolic Signatura give?"

"That the Pope approved the cardinals' decision *in forma specifica*. Therefore I will ask them to give me written proof of this approval *in forma specifica*.... We will see."

"This Is Why I Persist"

And during an evening spiritual conference during the month of June: "Dear seminarians, my final recourse was blocked by an order from above. This is an intrusion of the executive power in order to paralyze the judicial power. Although it is not contrary to the constitution of the Church, it is 'a denial of justice.' This is why I persist. 'Ecône is Ecône,' dear Canon Berthod told me. Therefore we will continue Ecône and the Society. First we will all go on pilgrimage to Rome at Pentecost to take an oath of fidelity to the Rome of all ages. And then, be back to the seminary, all of you, on September 15!"

Yes, almost all of them would return, but five professors, out of fear of "disobeying," left the seminary, in particular, alas, the two dear and excellent Dominicans, Fathers Mehrle and Spicq. It was a disappointment.

"But let us not linger and weep," the prelate in Ecône decided. "We will make good these losses!"

One example of Archbishop Lefebvre's counterattack:

"Dear Father Schmidberger," the founder said, "you are only a deacon, but I appoint you rector and professor of our new seminary in German-speaking Switzerland, in Weissbad, in the Canton of Appenzell!"

"At your service, *Monseigneur!*"

In autumn 1975, Cardinal Villot forbade all the bishops of the world to incardinate (enroll) Archbishop Lefebvre's seminarians in their diocese. Hence, if the "rebel" Archbishop ordained them priests without incardination, he incurred suspension *"a collatione ordinum"*: he would no longer be able to ordain any priest legitimately. Furthermore Archbishop Benelli, Cardinal Villot's substitute, expressly forbade Archbishop Lefebvre to proceed to the ordinations scheduled for June 1976, under pain of suspension *"a divinis"*: being deprived of his faculties to celebrate the sacraments and therefore to say Mass!

"If your seminarians are seriously prepared for priestly ministry in true fidelity to the *conciliar Church*," Benelli added, "we will make sure to find a solution for them."

"What is this conciliar Church?" said the Archbishop to his close collaborators. "What is this absolute innovation?"

CHAPTER XXIII

"The Hot Summer" of 1976

On this June 29, 1976, at 9:00 a.m., the procession started and made it way down the meadow in Ecône: the Archbishop, wearing miter and gloves, advances with cross in hand, his face a bit tense but determined. He will ordain thirteen priests and fourteen subdeacons despite Rome's orders not to do so.

Despite Rome's Prohibition ...

In Flavigny, two days before, Father Dhanis had come from Rome to beg him to "concelebrate the new Mass with him and then everything would be resolved," but the Archbishop had shown him the door. And that very day he showed the door to Cardinal Thiandoum also (whom he had ordained a priest in Dakar) who had come to beg him. He did not yield.

In his sermon he explained the reason for his resistance—a reason of faith:

"The New Mass is a symbol, an expression of a new and modernist faith. Throughout the centuries Holy Church has guarded this precious treasure of Holy Mass in its thousand-year-old rite as canonized, so to speak, by Saint Pius V. Why? Because this Mass contains all of our faith: faith in the divinity of our Lord Jesus Christ, faith in Redemption by our Lord Jesus Christ, faith in the Blood of our Lord Jesus Christ that was shed for the redemption of our sins!"

Might the Holy See Be Vacant?

On that day, the prelate incurred the two above-mentioned suspensions. Although severely struck by these censures for a moment,

133

he reacted humorously and energetically, in a polemical style that noticeably goes beyond his usual thinking.

"This suspension forbids me to say the New Mass! I am asked to obey the Conciliar Church. But this Conciliar Church is schismatic because it breaks with the Catholic Church of all time. It has its new dogmas (the dignity of the person), its new priesthood (the universal priesthood of the faithful), its new institutions (collegiality), its new worship (the cult of man)! The Council, turning its back on Tradition and breaking with the Church of the past, is a schismatic Council! Now heresy and schism can mean that a Pope never was or is no longer Pope! How can a Pope, the true successor of Peter, who is assured of the assistance of the Holy Ghost, preside over the most profound, the most extensive destruction of the Church in her history in such a short time? This is something that no heresiarch has ever succeeded in doing!"

This far-reaching question deserved to be asked. The Archbishop would pose it again several times: was it possible that this Pope is not the Pope? He always answered it with his usual practical wisdom, mistrusting the "abstract arguments that do not take all the circumstances into account."

"I prefer to think that these popes, legitimately elected and accepted by the whole Church, are true popes. Perhaps later on things will be revealed or will appear to us which ought to have been obvious and will be quite clear then, which will allow the Church to judge that such and such a Pope had not been one. But for the moment, in the absence of such evidence, I prefer to think that this Pope is Pope; I also want to keep up relations with the Holy See."

Following these explanations, some who were too simple-minded or too rigid would leave Archbishop Lefebvre, such as Father Guérard des Lauriers, O.P., intermittently a professor in Ecône, who would finally receive episcopal consecration from the hands of Archbishop Ngo Dinh Thuc, former Archbishop of Hué in Indochina; Bishop Guérard in turn would consecrate bishops for groups of priests who dissented from the Society of Saint Pius

X and were called "sedevacantists": they are convinced, they claim, for various reasons that the Holy See is vacant.

Unwanted Popularity

In that "hot summer" of 1976, hot because of the atmospheric temperature and because of the ardor of the combatants, the thermometer of Archbishop Lefebvre's popularity spiked. An opinion poll showed that 27% of Frenchmen "agreed" with his ideas, while 24% disapprove of them and the others had no opinion. The French Prime Minister, Jacques Chirac, worried about the Lefebvrist impact on the upcoming elections, wrote to the prelate on July 16 a tirade that was surprising for the head of government of an officially secular State.

"Catholic France, the eldest daughter of the Church by an immemorial privilege, has been able to remain attached to the Successor of Peter. Your genius will make you find words of reconciliation."

Did Chirac not know about the baptism of Rheims which, on Christmas Day, 496, made France the first Christian nation? Not by "privilege," not by an "immemorial" right but rather with the right of seniority!

On August 29, despite a new warning from Paul VI, the Archbishop celebrated a public Mass in the sports stadium of the trade fair in Lille, with a crowd of 7,000 Catholics and a media circus on the lookout for good one-liners hurled by the firebrand "suspended bishop."

"The Revolution," he said, "made martyrs, but that is nothing compared to what Vatican II has done: priests have apostatized from the priesthood! This marriage between the Church and Revolution brought about by Vatican II is an adulterous marriage. And this adulterous union can only produce illegitimate children. The new rite of Mass is an illegitimate rite, the sacraments are illegitimate sacraments, the priests who come from the seminaries are illegitimate priests.... Our Lord Jesus Christ is the only person in the world who can say 'I am God.' Therefore, He is the only king of humanity. There will be no peace on earth except through the reign of our Lord Jesus Christ. His reign—the reign of God's Commandments and of the Gospel—will bring about justice and peace. One sees this clearly in Argentina since they have had a government with principles and authority!"

Scribbling feverishly, the journalists noted the prelate's controlled skid: The praise of a dictatorship! *Monseigneur* continued at the same pace:

"I am with twenty centuries of the Church. People tell me, 'You are judging the Pope!' I am not the one judging the Pope; Tradition is. Archbishop Benelli threw in my face: 'You are not the one who makes truth!' Of course, I am not the one who makes truth, but neither is the Pope!"

A muted murmur welcomed these words, and one could see reporters leaving to phone in to their editors "the word of rupture." But the prelate explained himself:

"Our Lord Jesus Christ is the truth. Refer to our catechism. A five-year-old child with his catechism can tell his bishop a thing or two. If the bishop professes an error, who is right? The catechism!"

The Meeting with Paul VI

On September 11, 1976, in Castel Gandolfo, his summer residence, Paul VI finally agreed to receive Archbishop Lefebvre. The meeting was painful.

"You are destroying the Church!" Paul cried. "It is horrible! You stir up Christians against the Pope and against the Council! Doesn't your conscience reproach you with anything?"

"No, Holy Father."

"You are unconscious!"

"I am conscious of continuing the Church, Most Holy Father! Your Holiness has the solution in your hands. You allow many experiments to be made in the Church. Well, then, let us make the experiment of Tradition!"

Paul VI reflected for a few days, then confided his thought to Jean Guitton, a member of the French Academy, who tried to mediate:

"No, this 'Mass of Saint Pius V,' as they see it in Ecône, is becoming a symbol for condemning the Council. If it was tolerated by way of exception, the whole Council would be shaken!"

CHAPTER XXIV

The Council in Light of Tradition

"Do You Accept the Council, *Monseigneur?*"

On November 18, 1978, the new Pope John Paul II received Archbishop Lefebvre at the Vatican palace; Cardinal Seper, Prefect of the Sacred Congregation for the Doctrine of the Faith, was present. Former Archbishop of Zagreb, he suffered Communist persecutions. But since his arrival in Rome, he had become a persecutor, as we will see.

How Archbishop Lefebvre Hustles John Paul II

"Holy Father," Archbishop Lefebvre replied, "I would accept the formula of Your Holiness to the effect that 'the Council must be understood in light of sacred Tradition and on the basis of the constant Magisterium of the Church."

"Well, that's quite according to the norm. What about the present rite of the Mass?"

"Your Holiness only has to say one word to the bishops throughout the world: 'We authorize the free celebration of the rite that many centuries of Tradition have used for the sanctification of souls.' The dioceses would designate the places and the times that are reserved for it. The bishops would be astonished to find again in a few years a surge of devotion and sanctification that they thought had disappeared forever! Our priories would offer to the parishes the service of preaching missions and the Spiritual Exercises of Saint Ignatius, in full submission to the local Ordinaries."

But astonished by the optimism and the dynamism of the prelate from Ecône, Seper exclaimed: "Careful, Holy Father; they are making a flag out of this Mass!"

And they parted ways on this odd remark of the Pope, who did not like to be hustled or outclassed in traditionalism: "Stop it, *Monseigneur*, stop it, stop it!"

Bittersweet Exchanges with Cardinal Seper

Subsequently the Archbishop avoided a trial before the Sacred Office that Seper wanted to bring against him! The Cardinal accused him of rejecting the Council and of his "illegitimate" pastoral activities: confirmations and ordinations.

Rather than remain on the defensive, an attitude of inferiority, Archbishop Lefebvre gently hustled John Paul II once again, writing to him on April 25, 1979, still optimistic and positive:

"Our five seminaries could be ten or twenty tomorrow; our 170 major seminarians a thousand, if approval was granted, even provisionally. We could render an immense service to the bishops by preparing true priests for them, as Saint John Eudes, Saint Vincent de Paul and Blessed Olier did. Isn't is possible to grant us the status that is already in force in the personal prelatures, such as the Mission of France, whose Superior is a bishop? My successor, designated according to the statutes of the Society, would receive episcopal consecration. This is a very ancient custom in the Church, which has borne its fruits."

But Seper, when informed about this Lefebvre's new offensive in the art of persuasion, entrenched himself behind canonical impossibilities and disciplinary conditions. No good will was evident on Rome's part.

The prelate magnanimously insisted on June 23: "Do you want me to suspend ordinations? I agree to do so for six months. Do you fear that the decree that is being prepared to liberalize the Traditional Mass 'might appear as a victory of Ecône' (politicking);

well, that's very simple: once the liturgical problem is settled, the problem of Ecône will be solved easily!"

But Seper clung to the Council and to the prelate's illicit activities. He wrote to him acrimoniously on October 20, 1980, without the least pretense of *romanità*: "The Masses that you have celebrated again are for the most part sacrileges! Without any exaggeration! And you must adhere to the teachings of the Council 'understood in light of Tradition and based on the constant Magisterium,' as it seemed we had agreed on; and you must accept with a religious submission of will and intellect the points of the Council that are not defined as obligatorily held by the Church, each one according to its object and its style, as Cardinal Felici declared at the Council."

Then the Archbishop decided to explain his "formula of adherence" to Cardinal Seper. "The Council understood 'in light of Tradition' means 'according to the criterion of Tradition.' A criterion means a 'sieve,' it is like a colander: what passes through it is good; what does not pass is thrown away. The criterion of all Magisterial teaching is precisely its conformity with Tradition and with the constant Magisterium of the Church. What is not in conformity with it, we reject. Hence the serious reservations that must be had concerning some conciliar documents, like *Dignitatis humanae* on religious liberty and *Gaudium et spes* on the Church in the modern world."

On February 19, 1981, Seper replied, likewise in writing: "Your reservations about some of the conciliar documents should incite you instead to seek to understand the teachings of these documents and to integrate them into the centuries-old Tradition of the Church!"

The Dilemma

Archbishop Lefebvre, passing through Ecône, read this exchange of letters to the community.

Father Tissier, professor of the treatise on the Magisterium at Ecône, said to his colleagues: "There's a dilemma here. One of two things is true: either Tradition is indeed the 'criterion' for the truth or the errors of the Council, as *Monseigneur* says, or else the contrary: the Council—the present-day Magisterium—makes a rule that its teachings are to be integrated into the line of Tradition, as the Cardinal says."

What attitude is to be adopted then?

"The solution," Father Tissier suggested, "is that *Monseigneur* should first demonstrate that the Council *is not Magisterial*, by signs external and internal to the Conciliar documents, and then he will have the right to criticize the Council, to find errors in it which cannot be integrated into the continuity of Tradition!"

Is that impossible?

In November 1984, Archbishop Lefebvre read with alarm the excerpts from *The Ratzinger Report*—an interview granted by Cardinal Joseph Ratzinger, Seper's successor, to the journalist Vittorio Messori: "Why the Faith is in Crisis," published by the Italian monthly magazine *Jesus*. Here is what the Cardinal said:

"The problem in the Sixties was to acquire the best values expressed by two centuries of liberal culture; they originated outside the Church but can find their place—provided they are clarified and corrected—in her perspective on the world. This is what was done. It is true that the results disappointed hopes that were perhaps naive. This is why we need to find a new equilibrium."

Archbishop Lefebvre told his seminarians: "The Cardinal acknowledges that the crisis of the Church is due to this attempt by the Council to marry Catholic principles to 'liberal values'; to marry the Church with the Revolution; this is what I have always said! Such an attempt was doomed to failure. And the Cardinal admits this failure: 'We need to find a new equilibrium,' he says. But it is an impossible equilibrium!"

When he met the prelate in Rickenbach in 1985, the Secretary General of the Society asked: "*Monseigneur*, is this attempt Magisterial, is it the Magisterium?"

"That's one question that I did not ask; I considered the ambiguities, the errors in the documents, and above all the fruits: you remember that in 1966, when Cardinal Ottaviani surveyed the fruits of the Council, I replied: 'The Council promoted in an unimaginable way the spread of liberal errors,' and I explain how: 'The Council allowed those who professed the errors and the tendencies condemned by the popes to think legitimately that their doctrines were approved from now on.'"

"But *Monseigneur*, a Council that promotes heresy by no longer condemning errors, by marrying truth to error, is it the Magisterium of the Church?"

"I just touched on this question ten years later, in 1976, in my foreword to *I Accuse the Council*: "We can make the well-founded statement, by arguments both of external criticism and of internal criticism, that the spirit which dominated the Council and inspired so many of its ambiguous and even frankly erroneous texts was not that of the Holy Ghost."

"Of course, *Monseigneur*, the Holy Ghost does not intervene to 'inspire' a Council as He inspires the sacred authors of Sacred Scripture!"

"No, of course not; at the Council He assists the assembly to prevent error; He is the guarantor of infallibility. Now this Council, according to the intention of John XXIII, claimed to be 'pastoral' and, according to Archbishop Felici, Secretary General of the Council, 'avoided producing any document endowed with the note of infallibility.' Therefore errors could slip in, and hence it is legitimate to debate certain paragraphs of this Council: their orientation, their ambiguities and even errors, while admitting that some passages can provide fine meditations. One can judge this Council. This is what I explained to you, incidentally, ten years ago (in a spiritual conference, June 12, 1975)."

The Council's Magisterial Non-Authority

"*Monseigneur*," Father Tissier asked, "isn't there more than just the 'pastoral' character of the Council? It seems that the Holy Ghost was positively driven out. Isn't this 'spirit of the Council' what drove the Holy Ghost away, the spirit that the Council itself describes in *Gaudium et spes* and even declares as being its primary intention?"

"Tell me what you mean."

Father Tissier read to him: "'The Council intends first of all to assess those values which are most highly prized today and to relate them to their divine source. For such values, insofar as they stem from the natural talents given to man by God, are exceedingly good. Not seldom, however, owing to corruption of the human heart, they are distorted through lack of due order, so that they need to be set right.'"

"I missed that passage; indeed Cardinal Ratzinger last year merely cited that sentence from the Council. It was cut-and-paste!"

"Then allow me, *Monseigneur*: when a Council itself declares that its *primary intention* is to acquire, after being purified, so to speak, the liberal errors (that were condemned by the nineteenth-century popes), doesn't this constitute from the start an intention opposed to the very nature of the Magisterium of the Church?"

"It does seem so to me; the nature of the Magisterium is to keep and to transmit the truth of Our Lord and not to mix profane novelties into it, as Saint Paul says (I Tim. 6:20)."

"Then, *Monseigneur*, isn't this initial intention such as to block from the outset the assistance of the Holy Ghost, to derail the Council and to make of it a counter-Magisterium?"

"It is what the Cardinal himself in *The Principles of Catholic Theology* called 'a revision of the *Syllabus* of Pius IX, a kind of counter-syllabus.' The *Syllabus* is a collection of so-called liberal values condemned by the Church's Magisterium; therefore the Council with its 'counter-syllabus' seems to be a counter-magisterium."

"*Monseigneur*, one could say: The Holy Ghost was ready to descend upon the Assembly, but it seems to have sent Him away: 'Excuse us, this is not the right time; we are busy welcoming liberal values!'"

CHAPTER XXV

Sisters, Brothers and Schools 1972-1979

While rather tense relations were established between the Society and the Roman authorities, Divine Providence gave rise to a wide-ranging internal development.

The Help of Sister Marie-Gabriel Lefebvre

In 1972 the founder was in Australia during the Eucharistic Congress in Sydney, where during the procession the Bible was carried instead of the Blessed Sacrament. He remained aloof and met several families, friends of the Society, and some candidates for the priesthood....

"*Monseigneur*, could I enter your Sisters?"

This was not a candidate for the seminary, but a young woman whose open countenance and simple faith touched the Archbishop; Jeanine Ward asked admission to a congregation that does not exist!

"It exists in my head, this congregation, and it is even foreseen by the Statutes of our Priestly Society: 'Affiliated sisters, when God raised them up.'"

But how could they be formed? A co-foundress is necessary!

Sister Marie-Gabriel, a Holy Ghost nun, a nursing sister at the Stella Maris mission near Dakar, heard reports about the first misadventures of her brother Marcel Lefebvre with Rome. To the curate in Riddes, passing through Senegal on a lecture tour about Ecône, she asked: "What is my brother doing? People are talking about him; he has troubles with the Vatican!"

Later on, while spending a month in Switzerland to rest, she met her brother, who reassured her: "Troubles, no! But vocations, Bernadette! For the 'Sisters of the Society of Saint Pius X,' I need you. Ask your Superior General to release you and join me in Albano, near Rome. You will open the novitiate!"

Sold on the idea by her enterprising brother, Sister Marie-Gabriel set aside her uneasiness and launched into the adventure.

The Sisters of the Society of Saint Pius X

The founder was already composing a draft of the Sisters' Constitutions.

"They will be active and contemplative; they will be the auxiliaries of the priests in their apostolates. Just as the Mother of Jesus, through her Compassion, participated in the priestly work of Jesus dying on the Cross for the redemption of souls, so too the Sisters will have a special devotion to the Holy Sacrifice of the Mass and to the Eucharistic Victim; they will associate themselves to the presence of Mary Coredemptrix by the altar and at the foot of the Cross. This is why they will have an hour of adoration in the present of Jesus in the Host during the course of the day."

With Mother Marie-Gabriel, the Archbishop carefully designed the Sisters' habit, knowing how attentive they were to every detail of its composition, since the habit contains in itself the spirit of the religious institute, reflects its purpose and life. It would be a long black robe, covering the ankles, and equipped with a narrow belt of black cloth, a white bib with a collar will cover the top part of the robe and will be, like it, covered by a long black scapular, with a squared neckline; the head will be covered with a white bonnet with a discreet headband to which would be attached a simple, rather long black veil, whose vertical fold will point somewhat toward the top of the forehead.

This was a far cry from the ample religious habits of old, made of heavy cloth with wide sleeves and a double veil topping a cylindrical tiara or a bonnet whose headband went down to the eyebrows: cumbersome, certainly, and even penitential. Thus the founder assigned to his daughters a habit whose simplicity, practical adaptation and good taste are the distinguishing feature of their institute.

The Oblate Sisters of the Society

One fine day in 1973, the aunt of the seminarian Laurençon arrived in Ecône; she declared to the Rector: "Pray for a break-up!" She meant with the Superior of her congregation, which has become progressive. She remained in Ecône, becoming the first Oblate Sister of the Society: Sister Marie Bernard. Thus the Oblates were young girls or less young women who, without public vows but with a rule, seek to lead a religious life at the service of the Society.

The Brothers of the Society

Now one day in 1972, one year earlier, a spiritual son of Father Victor Alain Berto appeared at the door in Ecône: the future Brother Gabriel. Vietnamese, with his narrow eyes and his perpetual Asian smile, he used the seminary's new kitchen for the first time. Then came Brother Dominic, who was gifted with a fine singing voice; he would direct the schola of Saint Michael's School in France for more than forty years. Twenty years later an Argentine came to the seminary in La Reja, Brother John of the Cross: during the assault on the seminary by armed thieves, he heroically jumped outside from the window of his room. Then, fearing that he had sounded the alarm, the bandits fled, but not without knocking out the Rector, Father Lagneau, and firing a shot, whose impact remained imprinted on the cloister wall.

If, besides this spirit of devotion, the candidate brothers had particular talents or degrees, they could be instructors or teachers in the schools of the Society.

The Schools

Not far from Saint-Michel-en-Brenne, where the Sisters would soon settle, in its little church in Vineuil, on the edge of the Champagne Berrichonne region and near the ponds of La Brenne, Father Luneau, like many courageous priests throughout the world, attracted every Sunday a little crowd of Catholics who were devoted to the true Mass. That day he was praying his breviary in the garden of the rectory when two gentlemen walked into it:

"Father Curate, our boys need a confessor. Our Saint Michael's School is Catholic."

And the kindly little priest became chaplain in Châteauroux, professor of chant, literature, Latin and Greek. But he decided to change things:

"Gentlemen," he declared one day to Messieurs Mazure and Soulet, "there has to be a priest here as principal of this school. Think of Don Bosco!"

"Well, well, Father! Do we have to retire?"

"No, not at all. Keep teaching but ask Archbishop Lefebvre for a priest!"

And the arrangements were made for the beginning of the school year in 1979.

In Alsace-Lorraine, a bearded Capuchin, Father Rohmer, was the one who asked for a "successor" to head his apprentices. They would be replaced by scholars who would soon have as their principal a young "priest from Ecône" at "Morning Star," with the continuation of the night-time prayer vigils of the zealous faithful, even from Germany: *"Maria zu lieben ist es mir meine Zier!"* "To love Mary is my glory," from an old Marian hymn. Beyond the Rhine River, Father Schmidberger sent his compatriot Father Michael Wildfeuer (the name means "wildfire") to Sarrebrück to found Saint Arnual school for boys, and then in central Germany the "Don Bosco Schule": an eighteenth-century castle surrounded by water, nicknamed the *Wasserschloss*, or Water Castle; with an immense school adjoining it; Father Schmidberger purchased both buildings.

Archbishop Lefebvre commented: "Well! And here I appointed Father Schmidberger as a hardworking man, certainly, but thrifty, like every self-respecting Swabian; now look at the spendthrift!"

This was just an admiring joke, for isn't the virtue of magnificence, of being able to make large expenses advisedly, 'magnos sumptus,' a virtue of the missionary Archbishop and builder himself?

But what would the prelate say when Father Bolduc, Superior of the Southwest District in the United States, purchased a university! Saint Mary's College, in Kansas, was indeed a famous high school or preparatory school of the Jesuit Fathers, popularized by the novels of Francis Finn, and extended by the first two years of university, or "college" as Americans call it, and equipped with a marvelous Gothic chapel with splendid stained-glass windows; this precious monument, alas, later perished in a fire.

These Catholic schools, just like the families who accepted the financial sacrifices required to send their boys to them, were fertile ground where many priestly and religious vocations were and still are awakened.

"I rejoice," the Archbishop said, "to observe there the same fruits that, in its day, were produced by my old Sacred Heart College in Tourcoing."

"*Monseigneur*," Father Aulagnier asked, "sum up for us your directives for the Society's schools."

Here they were: "Our Catholic schools must be truly Catholic. Their purpose is to instill religion in the children. Often adults are afraid to demand too much of young people, but that is an error. It is necessary to push and to drive children to piety."

"A Catholic school is a school where you learn to be disciplined, where you learn sacrifice. If not, we cannot devote ourselves, give ourselves, be truly charitable. We discipline our intellect by receiving the truth, by submitting it to the truth of the natural realities, to the truth also of Our Lord Jesus Christ."

"We also discipline our will by fighting against our bad tendencies which come from original sin. But there is need of grace; this is why at the center of the school there is the chapel and Holy Mass, which is its heart. The educator can do nothing without the action of sanctifying grace in the soul of the pupil."

"The purpose of our schools is to form a Catholic elite and not to be reform schools [for delinquents]!"

"The teaching of history is of capital importance. One cannot study history except from the perspective of the event of the Incarnation: everything flows from Our Lord Jesus Christ, and everything leads to Him."

CHAPTER XXVI

In America
1977-1984

South America and Mexico

"What was that?" the Archbishop exclaimed, interrupted by a brouhaha during his conference.

"A bomb, *Monseigneur*! It was about to explode in the cloak-room when they defused it!"

Father Jean Michel Faure, newly ordained in June 1977, had seen others: "Oh, *Monseigneur*, in Algeria I confronted National Liberation Front agents who set bombs; I'm used to counter-revolutionary combat!"

These were the turbulent conditions in which, on November 27, the priory and seminary San Pio X would be founded in Buenos Aires, in a large house on Venezuela Street that was generously placed at the Society's disposal; the first four recruits from South America would enter it, among them Alfonso de Galarreta. Soon the seminary would move to the *"campo"* [countryside], to La Reja, beneath a hangar made of corrugated iron, freezing in the winter and torrid in the summer, then in sober, pleasant buildings in the Spanish colonial style that the prelate would have built there.

But earlier in July, Father Faure went ahead of him to Mexico. Archbishop Lefebvre joined him on the ninth in Texas, where he blessed the large parish acquired in Dickinson by Father Bolduc.

In Bogota, Colombia, the joust with the press people began: a mob of journalists waited for *Monseigneur* at the airport; the prelate's car was accompanied everywhere by fifteen military men and some members of the secret police.... In the streets, radio reporters

153

followed him and announced: "Archbishop Lefebvre is now on 45th Avenue." The people cried: *"Viva Monseñor!"* and knelt to receive his blessing.

In Santiago, Chile, on July 17, the Archbishop heard from the plane the crowd shouting: *"Lefebvre, sí! Communismo, no!"* It was impossible to force one's way through them; escorted by two police cars, the Archbishop's vehicle left the airport along trails. The newspaper headlines read: "Cardinal Silva Henriquez says: Lefebvre is a Judas." But the next edition corrected it: "Lefebvre replies: I am no Judas; I did not kiss Fidel Castro!"

United States and Canada

In the United States, where the apostolate of the true Mass had developed admirably, along with schools for boys, there were difficulties of another sort in 1982. At the headquarters of the Society in the United States, in Oyster Bay near New York, Father Clarence Kelly decided: "Pope John Paul II preaches that 'every human being, through the Incarnation of the Son of God, is redeemed from his mother's womb.' He's a heretic, and therefore he is not Pope!"

Father Donald Sanborn, at the seminary in Ridgefield, thought for his part: "Archbishop Lefebvre wants to impose on us the liturgical reform of John XXIII, the one in 1962. Now this reform is liberal. Let us keep the rites of Pius XII, or rather of Saint Pius X!"

With them, a group of nine priests seceded in 1983. In response to this emergency, Father Richard Williamson was sent from Ecône to the United States so as to keep Ridgefield and its seminarians. He told them: "We have no authority to decide that the Pope is not legitimate or that the See of Saint Peter is vacant; this is a misguided battle. Our job is to keep the faith and to resist the conciliar errors. As for the 1962 liturgical reform, it is along the lines of the reform by Saint Pius X."

In Shawinigan, Canada, young Father Simpson, whom Archbishop Lefebvre sent into the snows of New France in 1979, had a doubt: "Do I really have the right to keep the old Mass? Pope Paul VI declared in 1976 that 'the new rite instituted in the implementation of Vatican Council II was introduced in order to replace the old one.' For a clear insight on this, I will write to Sister Lucia in Fatima, who has lights from heaven!"

And of course, Sister Lucia replied that one must obey the Pope. Apart from her mission as messenger of the Immaculate Heart of Mary, she had no special lights. Then Father Simpson left the priory and the Society.

Africa Again!

In Gabon, in Africa, the opposite would be the case: In 1985, the zealous Father Patrick Groche had no doubts at all. Right after getting off the plane, he declared to Bishop François Ndong, the retired Bishop of Oyem (and a former student of Father Marcel and his vicar): "We have come to set up a house!"

But the budding missionary's visa was late in arriving. Fortunately the African wisdom of François Ndong came to the rescue: "Let *Monseigneur* Lefebvre come to talk to the President of the Republic!"

Monseigneur came, wearing his dear white cassock and his Spiritan cincture. In February 1986, the veteran missionary met Omar Bongo, a former student of the Spiritans who had then converted to Islam.... Bongo told the Archbishop in African diplomatic language: "But, *Monseigneur,* no one ever said that Archbishop Lefebvre is a *persona non grata!*"

So it was settled! The trunks of Father Groche and of his acolyte, Deacon Stehlin, could be unpacked. The *Mission Saint-Pie* opened in La Peyrie.

Taking Stock of an Unexpected Expansion

Over the course of the years, Archbishop Lefebvre was able to multiply the "Districts," the "Autonomous Houses" and the seminaries of his Society. Let us count the seminaries: after Ecône

(1970) came Armada, near Detroit in the United States (1973), which then moved to Ridgefield, Connecticut (1975), and emigrated later to Winona, Minnesota, to a jewel of a Dominican novitiate from the 1950's, and finally to Dillwyn, Virginia, to a brand-new fortress of pink bricks and black slate roofs. Then came Weissbad in the canton of Appenzell in Switzerland (1975), which moved in 1977 to Zaitzkofen in Bavaria, to an eighteenth-century Baroque castle. Finally, La Reja was founded in 1982 in the countryside near Buenos Aires. Next would come Flavigny, in France, in the historical "Lacordaire House," and Holy Cross, in Australia, in a former Catholic secondary school, both founded by his successor at the head of the Society.

Indeed, the General Chapter of the Society, meeting in Ecône in July of 1982, elected a "Vicar General" for Archbishop Lefebvre, in the person of the German mathematician Franz Schmidberger. The latter called to the General House in Rickenbach, Swiss Canton of Solothurn, a young priest from Valais, Father Bernard Fellay, as Econome General.

Archbishop Lefebvre in fact had wisely decided to resign from his position as Superior General, so as to make sure with his own eyes that his institute functioned correctly under his successor.

In 1984 the Society of Saint Pius numbered 205 seminarians, and 119 priests who work in 48 houses and secondary schools for boys, distributed through twelve countries. To them the founder explained the spirit of this *Reconquista* [reconquering]:

"By contemplating Our Lord on the cross, in seeing there the summit of God's love driven to make the supreme Sacrifice, we will be missionaries through the desire to spread the Blood of Jesus Christ upon souls; this is the *mysterium fidei* [mystery of faith] to contemplate and to actualize, the priestly work par excellence. And the faithful will gather around us because of the Holy Sacrifice of the Mass, not for anything else."

"It is necessary to have absolute confidence in the position that we have adopted, because it is the attitude of the Church. It is not mine: it is not '*Monseigneur* Lefebvre's,' it is the Church's. One day or another, all the rest will collapse."

"I want to be fully in the spirit of the Church. I am convinced that in order to continue the Church, it is necessary to maintain the firmness of the faith in priestly formation. This is why I pursue this work without hesitating, despite the opposition that we meet even from the highest authorities of the Church."

CHAPTER XXVII

Scandals at the Top –
An Episcopal Consecration?
1979-1988

"I just read the first Encyclical by our Polish Pope. Listen to this: 'The Son of God by His Incarnation united Himself in a way to every human being.' Where in this is our incorporation with Jesus Christ through Baptism?"

The Professors Questioned by the Founder

In the cloister in Ecône, as the seminarians leave the midday meal, the prelate questioned his professors, who every time appreciate their founder's candor and the exchange of ideas that he frequently offers to them. And so they made use of a healthy freedom to present to him their views about current events and the questions of faith that they call into play.

"*Monseigneur*," the rector of the seminary replied, "all this is in Karl Rahner, and also in the Council: in *Gaudium et spes*!"

"And this other sentence: 'Man must appropriate the reality of the Incarnation and of redemption in order to find himself and to be amazed by it'?"

"That," says the professor of dogmatic theology, "is Father de Lubac, in his *Catholicisme*, which was censured under Pius XII! For if he 'finds himself' it is because 'man' and therefore every human being is already touched by the Incarnation and redemption before Baptism, even before his conception. Baptism only causes him to appropriate what he already is in a certain way. Or else . . ."

"I am fed up with this modern, unintelligible style; people are disgusted with it! Where is the simple, luminous, supernatural style of the Church's faith?"

The Enlarged Ecumenism of Pope John Paul II

"*Monseigneur*," the professor of ecclesiology asked two years later, "what are we to think about the 'Message to the Peoples of Asia' read in Manila by the Pope on February 21 (1981). His foggy thought is becoming clearer. May I quote him?

"'In the Holy Spirit, every person and every people have become, through the cross and resurrection of Christ, children of God, sharers in the divine nature and heirs of eternal life.'"

"This 'message' gives me to understand quite simply that the Church has a Pope who is destroying the Church. The situation of a Church governed by such a Pope, doesn't it legitimize the consecration of a bishop in order to provide for ordinations in the Society after God calls me home?"

Eventually Father Aulagnier told him, "Remember the letter that Father Calmel wrote to you in 1974: 'You will be compelled, *Monseigneur*, sooner or later, to consecrate a bishop so that your work might continue!'"

"Yes, and no bishop would agree now to ordain our seminarians...."

In an interview with André Figuéras, published in *Monde et Vie* on June 12, 1981, he explained his position: "If the situation in the Church worsened, if Providence shows me in an obvious way that I must do it, then no doubt I will resign myself to consecrating a bishop, since I can do so validly. But it would be an act of rupture with Rome—and that prospect is frightening people there, moreover—and I will do all I can to avoid it."

By "rupture" the prelate meant an apparent schism. But by no means a true rupture of communion with the Pope in his capacity as Vicar of Christ. But was John Paul II acting as Vicar of Christ in the spring of 1984? In Korea on May 6, the Pope addressed a "special greeting to the members of the Buddhist tradition who are preparing to celebrate the coming of Lord Buddha"; on May 10, he visited a Buddhist temple in Thailand, removed his shoes and sat at the feet of a bonze who is himself seated with his back to an altar on which there is a large statue of Buddha; in Geneva, during his visit to the headquarters of the World Council of Churches, he participated in a "liturgy of the Word" in the chapel of the WCC and reaffirmed that "the commitment of the Catholic Church in the ecumenical movement is irreversible." An ecumenism that was ceaselessly enlarging.

Moreover, the preceding year, on January 23, 1983, the same Pope John Paul II published a new Code of Canon Law (the Church's law). The laws of the Church were overturned: the "people of God" came before the hierarchy, the Pope is Pope because he is the head of the episcopal college; the members of the people of God all participate in their way in the priesthood of Christ; the Protestants can receive Holy Communion if they believe in the Real Presence.

"Here," Archbishop Lefebvre objected, "are many ambiguities and errors on essential points, which promote heresy. We cannot accept this new legislation wholesale."

"But," the professor of fundamental theology objected, "can a Pope, who is in principle infallible, promulgate errors and permit sacrileges by a universal law? The Pope enjoys the promises of Our Lord to Saint Peter: 'Thou art Peter and upon this rock I will build my Church, and the gates of hell will not prevail against it!' (Mt. 16:18). Therefore it is impossible for this new canon law to be detrimental to the faith!"

Archbishop Lefebvre answered: "You have to have lived from 1960 to this day in order to know that the popes can lead the Catholic Church to ruin! It seemed impossible to us, given the promises of the assistance of the Holy Spirit. But *contra factum non fit argumentum*: arguments have no validity against the facts. We must conclude that Our Lord, in pronouncing these words about assistance until the end of time, did not rule out periods of darkness and a time of Passion for the Church, His Mystical Bride!"

"I Am Waiting for Signs from Providence"

Now the Archbishop was advancing in years; at age 77 he experienced fatigue, he had fits of coughing that worried the seminarians: "Let's hope that *Monseigneur* lasts until my ordination!"

"All right!" he replied. "I am seriously thinking about a consecration; but I am waiting for signs from Providence, three very clear signs."

Right on time, shortly after the new Code of Canon Law, a second "sign" arrived: the announcement made by John Paul II on January 25, 1986, about an interreligious meeting for peace, in the city of Saint Francis, in Assisi.

Archbishop Lefebvre reacted: "I was sure that he would do something like that: like the 'multicolored congress' of religions that was held in Chicago from September 11 to 28, 1893, in the presence of Cardinal Gibbons, and other American Catholic bishops and priests, which Pope Leo XIII condemned on September 8, 1895. It's diabolical," he adds. "It is an insult to our Lord Jesus Christ! To whom will they pray for peace? The only God is the One who took flesh: '*Et Verbum caro factum est*': 'And the Word, God the Son, was made flesh'!"

On April 29, 1986, Dom Gérard Calvet, Prior of the Benedictines of Le Barroux, found the prelate's reaction exaggerated: "It is scandalous, no doubt, but not formally heretical to gather the leaders of various religions to have them pray to God, each in his own way, for peace!"

Archbishop Lefebvre obviously did not allow this "each in his own way": The "way" of the Protestants is to suppress the "Great Prayer" instituted by God, the Sacrifice of the Mass. Furthermore it was not about "praying to God' in various ways but rather about "no praying to the one true God," the God who reigns in the heavens, the God who became man, the God-man who still immolates Himself on the altar!

Alas, on October 27, 1986, the multicolored meeting took place and the motley procession of "religions" wound its way through the streets of Assisi.

On December 2, Archbishop Lefebvre and Bishop de Castro Mayer protested publicly: "The public sin against the one true God, against the first article of the Creed and the First Commandment of God causes us to tremble in horror: John Paul II encouraging the false religions to pray to their gods! The inconceivable impiousness, the insupportable humiliation for the Incarnate Word, for His Immaculate Mother, for His Church; a scandal with incalculable effects: on live television, millions or Christians will see the Vicar of Jesus Christ on an equal footing with the representatives of the false gods! If they allow that, they will lose the faith!"

The sedevacantist temptation (to declare that the Pope is not Pope and that the See of Peter is vacant: *Sedes vacans* in Latin) brushed by him in his Easter sermon in 1986, but he did not succumb to it; yet wasn't Assisi the clear indication that he could proceed to an episcopal consecration without the approval of such a Pope?

"It Would Be a Schism!" "No! It Will Not Be a Schism!"

The seminaries of Flavigny and Zaitzkofen were severely shaken by this possibility. A professor from his seminary in Albano, the Frenchman Philippe Le Pivain, wrote him in 1982 that "it would be to usurp a prerogative of the Supreme Pastor and there would be a rupture in the apostolic succession: the bishop consecrated would be an illegitimate bishop." The Rector of Zaitzkofen, the Swiss Josef Bisig, Second Assistant General, wrote to him in 1983 that such a consecration "would be a schism, a practical denial of the supreme power of the Pope," and now he clearly manifested his disagreement.

In Ecône, on the other hand, the Rector demonstrated, with the support of historical examples, that "the explicit intervention of the Holy See in the institution of a bishop is not required by divine right but only by the sacred canons, which are of simple ecclesiastical right."

Thus, Saint Eusebius of Samosata, on returning from his exile to Egypt at the time of the Arian heresy, while passing through Palestine consecrated Catholic bishops for the Church that had been devastated by the heresy, but without having in that province the authority of a Metropolitan, which is required by the sacred canons.

Commenting on that saving act of the holy bishop, Dom Adrien Gréa wrote in his book *L'Église et sa divine constitution* [*The Church and her Divine Constitution*]: "In order to make it legitimate, it was necessary that the very existence of the religion was at stake, that the ministry of the particular pastors was annihilated and that one could not hope for any possible recourse to the Holy See."

Archbishop Lefebvre simply observed that these three conditions were satisfied. The third was the moral impossibility of making John Paul II understand the situation of necessity (the state of emergency) that he himself was creating in the Church.

A Global Judgment and Some Necessary Clarifications

But the prelate in Ecône was often content to judge the situation globally, as he already did in November 1983 in a note written in his handwriting in the margin of the study by Father Bisig: "The problem of the situation of the faithful and of the situation of the current papacy renders moot the difficulties of jurisdiction, of disobedience and of apostolicity, because these notions presuppose a Pope who is Catholic in his faith, in his governing."

The Archbishop did not think as Dom Gérard does, that it was necessary to wait until John Paul II had professed a clear heresy and that one can then conclude that he had lost his power of jurisdiction; no, that was not the problem.

The question, he said, was that "we are indeed forced to observe that this Pope does not conduct himself as a Catholic, that he causes people to lose the faith, because his 'heresy in action' is more perceptible than a formally professed heresy; it insidiously destroys the faith of believers, it leads priests astray and it destroys the Church. The result is that without a faithful bishop, believers will be deprived of the faithful and assuredly valid priesthood."

Archbishop Lefebvre was simply pragmatic, practical common-sense in person. In order to prevent a schism, it remained for him to explain the functions of the bishop or bishops whom he would consecrate:

"They would be my auxiliaries, without any jurisdiction and only in order to administer confirmations and ordinations. It is absolutely not a question of making a 'parallel Church.' The purpose is simply to continue the Society, so that it might not die out. The day when Rome returns to the profession of the truth of the Church of all ages, these bishops will place their episcopal dignity into the hands of the Pope: 'Here we are at your disposal.'"

CHAPTER XXVIII

Roman Negotiations – Decision to Consecrate Bishops 1985-1988

Thus since 1981, Archbishop Lefebvre had been speaking publicly about the possibility of consecrating a bishop. To some prevaricating journalists gathered in Roissy on December 19, 1982, he himself posed the question frankly:

"No doubt you will ask me if I am going to make bishops. Even so, I think that apparently it would be an act of rupture with Rome, which would be serious. I say it again: 'apparently,' because I think that in God's sight it is possible that my gesture would be a necessary act for the history of the Church, for the continuation of the Church, of the Catholic priesthood. So I am not saying that I won't do it someday, but only in even more tragic circumstances."

From 1981 to 1984, Rome was increasingly "under pressure"; faced with the threat of a Society of Saint Pius X that had become uncontrollable by the Roman authority, Rome invoked the crushing argument: "It would be a schism!"

Cardinal Ratzinger as Mediator

After a plenary meeting of the cardinals in the Curia, Cardinal Ratzinger was delegated to settle the matter: Rome would yield about the bishop demanded by Lefebvre, and Archbishop Lefebvre will have to yield about the Council. In January 1985 the two prelates met in Rome.

"*Monseigneur*, ask; ask for all that you want!"

"Even if I ask you for the consecration of an auxiliary bishop? Your Eminence, even if you grant us that, with the traditional liturgy, with our seminaries and ordinations according to the traditional rite, with some autonomy with regard to the diocesan bishops, we do not have the same principles! Look: 1) We will be entering a framework that will 'normalize' us, will give us a legal status; but we will be commanded by authorities who are against what we do! 2) Against what we teach our seminarians, too. If our seminarians adopt these ideas, they no longer have a place in our seminaries! 3) Furthermore, we will give the impression of vouching for the very things that are destroying the Church. What situation will we be in then, Your Eminence?"

But Archbishop Lefebvre was not "completely of one mind"; he said to his close co-workers: "If I set my conditions in order to protect us on these three points ... And since the Cardinal no longer seems to demand that we accept the Council, it is worth discussing the matter inch by inch with the Holy See: That they might recognize us just as we are, without trying to change us!"

Was this realistic? Certainly Rome is Rome, but it is a neo-Modernist Rome: that was the reality.

Later on, after the Archbishop's death, Cardinal Ratzinger would say: "Every time traditionalist communities have drawn closer to the Holy See and have entered into full communion with the Church, we have observed in them a development toward an understanding of the Council and of the reforms...."

Differing Attitudes in the Family of Tradition

As for the faithful Traditional Catholics, the opinions ran the gamut and differed considerably.

A certain Michel Martin (pen name for Professor Georges Salet) wrote in *De Rome et d'ailleurs*: "Traditionalism must not commit suicide! If obliged to choose between the Church of John Paul II and the dissident Church, the vast majority of Traditionalists would break solidarity with Archbishop Lefebvre!"

Dom Gérard Calvet, for his part, thought it prudent to warn: "Careful! Let us flee the sectarian spirit, let us not form a 'little Church' like the French Catholics after the Revolution who rejected the bishops designated by Bonaparte and appointed by Rome! They never returned to the Church! Let us trust the Holy Father!"

In a diametrically opposite view, a "Catholic from Saint-Nicolas-du-Chardonnet from the first day" called for "the firm, helpful conduct of an episcopate that is always renewed and always faithful."

"Who can give us this episcopate, *Monseigneur*," he wrote, "without breaking the chain that unites us to Saint Peter, if not you?"

Rome Stubbornly Insists on Professing the Religious Liberty of the Human Person

Archbishop Lefebvre still hesitated ... when he received from Rome the response to the *dubia*, to the doubts that he presented to the Holy See about the conciliar teaching on *religious liberty*. The response was fifty pages long; the Archbishop immediately saw its flaw.

"The human person, they tell us, has a vital space of autonomy in which, by reason of his dignity, he can act publicly in religious matters without the State being able to intervene."

But he replied: "There is no area in which the State is incompetent (where it would not be its role) to intervene with regard to public human acts in society. For such acts involve morality which is subject either to edification or to scandal: in other words, a good example like the one that is given by the Catholic Mass, celebrated openly, or on the contrary an occasion for falling outside of the faith, like the one that is given by Protestant worship likewise held openly in a Catholic society (*civitas*). If the State deems it preferable to support the scandal, it acts according to the tolerance spoken of by Saint Augustine, Saint Thomas and the Magisterium down to Pope Pius XII: In doing so, the State does not recognize an innate right belonging to the innovators or the dissidents, but tolerates them so as to avoid a war of religion, and it agrees to guarantee them this liberty by a civil right." "The altogether unsatisfactory response to the *dubia*," said Archbishop Lefebvre, "is for me the third Providential 'sign' in favor of an episcopal consecration."

He told the seminarians: "Rome is in apostasy (it gives up the profession of the Catholic faith). Rome no longer thinks that the civil authority can and must protect the Church of Our Lord Jesus Christ against heresies. The State is said to be 'incompetent (*i.e.* it is not its role) to judge in matters of religion,' as Father John Courtney Murray wrongly claimed and Bishop De Smedt, the reporter of the schema, repeated to the Council. That is false; those who govern are capable and owe it to themselves to recognize the true religion and therefore to protect it."

Archbishop Lefebvre's Unexpected Change of View

Nevertheless, in Fatima on August 22, 1987, where the family of Tradition was celebrating the 70th anniversary of the apparitions of the Blessed Virgin, and where the Archbishop consecrated Russia to the Immaculate Heart of Mary, *Monseigneur* Lefebvre decided, in the presence of his close collaborators, to postpone the consecration, to try everything possible to obtain the bishop in complete submissive agreement with the Holy See, and in order to do that, to propose to Rome a type of structure called "personal Ordinariate" (a worldwide diocese of persons, without a particular territory) for the Society, the Superior of which would be a member of the Society appointed by the Pope, and furthermore the creation of a Roman Secretariat for the family of Tradition, and the visitation of the works of Tradition by Canadian Cardinal Édouard Gagnon.

"Cardinal Ratzinger," he said, "is no longer setting a condition for an agreement, yet it is taking so long that I demand that Rome be better acquainted with our works!"

Roman Negotiations, Protocol for an Agreement

Negotiations between Ratzinger and the Archbishop took place in Rome in April and May 1988. But the Cardinal, as though in passing, revealed the Roman intention: "I would be very glad to see," he says, "a parish Mass too at Saint-Nicolas-du-Chardonnet!"

Father Benoît Duroux, O.P., arms outstretched, went one better: "There is only one Church, *Monseigneur!*"

The Archbishop remained silent, then, at the 2:00 p.m. break, confided to his two assistants, Fathers Laroche and Tissier de Mallerais: "It's over. Let's stop. You heard what he said: the cohabitation of two rites, the Mass of all ages side by side with the new liturgy! That is what Rome wants to make us accept!"

Nevertheless the negotiations continued and concluded, on May 5, 1988, with a doctrinal and practical agreement: Archbishop Lefebvre had to commit himself in writing to "observe the new canon law" (the set of new laws of the Church) and to have "a positive attitude of study" concerning the points of the Council that "cause him difficulties," and the Pope would consider the appointment of a bishop, a member of the Society.

The Cardinal agreed orally "as long as the consecration can take place before the end of the Marian Year," in other words before August 15, 1988.

The next day, satisfied without actually being so, the prelate from Ecône, who did not sleep the whole night, demanded the acceptance in writing of the date of June 30; and a little later he demanded "the majority in the Roman Commission" and "three bishops." Rome did not quash anything right away, but the Cardinal, in the name of the Pope, would reply in the negative on May 30, while furthermore demanding other dossiers of candidates for the episcopacy "so that the Holy Father can freely choose a candidate having the profile called for in the protocol of agreement dated May 5."

The Meeting in Pointet

On May 30, 1988, at Notre Dame Priory in Pointet, Archbishop Lefebvre held a meeting of the "heads" of the Traditional family: the priests—Father Coache, Father André; the superiors of the men's and women's religious communities—Mérigny, Morgon, Le Barroux and La Font-de-Perthus, Brignoles, Fanjeaux, the Carmelites and the Sisters of the Society of Saint Pius X. He consulted them.

Father Lecareux, the Capuchins, Father Coache and Father Tissier de Mallerais (one of the episcopal candidates) declared that they were in favor of the agreement. Dom Gérard, Prior of the Benedictines of Le Barroux likewise: "If a rupture were to occur," he said, "we would become sociologically a sect, like the 'little Churches' from which not one ever returns to the universal Church. It is up to us to defend ourselves! Let us not underestimate our strength, which is doctrinal; and let us sign among ourselves a Charter of charity, a Catholic pact to do nothing to break our common front or to cause disagreement among the brethren."

But he would break this pact after the consecrations. . . .

The contrary position was expressed by Father André, the Dominican Sisters of Brignoles, those of Fanjeaux, the Sisters of the Society of Saint Pius X and the Carmelites, as well as Father Paul Aulagnier, First Assistant of the Society of Saint Pius X, who spelled out, in his personal way, the objective dangers of an agreement in disagreement.

"In Rome their theological and philosophical thought is contrary to the thought of the Church. I am afraid of this agreement; I fear the cunning of the devil, of the enemy. I do not see myself discussing with a Cardinal Lustiger, with a Cardinal Decourtray, with the Pope of Assisi. The bishop who is consecrated will have no moral authority in Rome. I fear the Roman bureaucracy, in which we will not take part. I adhere to Catholic Rome; I reject Modernist Rome, which threatens to be the Leviathan that devours us."

Archbishop Lefebvre then set forth his prudential judgment, inspired by his faith, taking the circumstances into account. "The atmosphere of the dialogues, the reflections of our interlocutors, show us that the Holy See's desire is to lead us to the Council and to its reforms, to bring us too into the embrace of the 'conciliar Church.' Hence, do the 'advantages'—which are the canonical normalization of our works, the guarantee of the Traditional liturgy and of the formation of our members, easier missionary contacts to convert priests and the lay faithful to Tradition, finally a bishop consecrated with the approval of the Holy See—do all these things enter into the assessment?"

And, the second horn of the dilemma: "If is necessary above all to preserve the Traditional family in order to maintain its cohesiveness and strength in the faith and in grace, considering that the purely formal tie with Modernist Rome cannot be weighed in the balance with the protection of this family, which is what remains of the true Catholic Church?"

To ask that question is to answer it, and on June 6, 1988, Archbishop Lefebvre wrote to John Paul II, in a style that is frank and, it must be said, not very kind:

"Given the refusal to consider our requests, and since it is obvious that the purpose of the reconciliation is not at all the same for the Holy See and for us, we think it preferable to await more propitious times for the return of Rome to Tradition."

CHAPTER XXIX

The Most Magnanimous Act
June 30, 1988

Throughout the radiant summer morning, June 30, 1988, five thousand Catholics crowded the meadow in Ecône beside the tent where ordinations were performed the previous day. Archbishop Lefebvre was going to proceed, against the Pope's will, to consecrate four priests of the Society bishops: Bernard Tissier de Mallerais, Richard Williamson, Alfonso de Galarreta and Bernard Fellay; and Bishop de Castro Mayer had traveled from Campos to be the co-consecrator.

Inevitably the media headlines already read: "The Schism," "The Rift," "The Schismatic Act of the Rebel Bishop."

"So That the Church Might Continue"

In an animated, sometimes moving tone of voice, Archbishop Lefebvre justified his action: "I seem to hear the voice of all these popes since Gregory XVI, Pius IX, Leo XIII, Saint Pius X, Benedict XVI, Pius XI, Pius XII saying to us: 'But for heaven's sake, what will you do with our teachings, with our preaching, with the Catholic faith? Will you abandon it? Will you let it disappear from this earth? For heaven's sake, for heaven's sake continue to guard this treasure that we gave you. Do not abandon the faithful, do not abandon the Church! Continue the Church! For in short, since the Council, what we condemned is now what the Roman authorities adopt and profess!'"

In turn, Bishop de Castro Mayer declared in a few words: "I want to manifest my sincere and profound adherence to the position of His Excellency Archbishop Lefebvre, dictated by his fidelity to the Church of all ages. We two drank from the same source, which is that of the Holy, Catholic, apostolic and Roman Church."

Then the Archbishop's face relaxed, his eyes lit up, his heart expanded: "This is quite true. I am not alone! The Church is the one who acts this morning, she indeed is the one who inspires and supports me, carries me in all the gestures that I must make. For almost two weeks my head has been pounding day and night...."

At the end of the ceremony, he confided to his assistants in the sacristy: "I thought that I would not get to the end of it."

But a moment ago, when he put the miter on the head of each of his four sons, all the witnesses noticed a radiant prelate, whose face was lit up with a victorious smile. The calm firmness of the previous day—when he showed the door to his friend, Jean Guitton, a member of the Académie Française, and refused the limousine sent to Ecône by a messenger from Rome to take him away from his entourage and bring him to the Vatican—was followed by a profound joy which would support his exhausted body the whole day.

The prelate did not proceed to the consecrations in agitation or anxiety. The rules for the discernment of spirits allow us to infer, behind that calm cheerfulness, the peace of a good conscience and to judge, albeit indirectly, the moral goodness of the act that was performed.

With the humor that never failed him even in the most serious hours, he said: "It is odd that some say that I yielded to pressure from my entourage in order to perform this act, when I was the one who had to push my collaborators to take this step with me!"

He knew that he incurred a so-called "excommunication" and that Rome would declare this consecration a "schismatic act." But he responded in advance to those insults. Henceforth, during the three years that God would grant him, he would accompany with his moral presence his four young auxiliaries, allowing them from now on to perform ordinations, at which he assists modestly, following with an ardent glance the gestures of his sons as they in turn transmit the priesthood.... While Archbishop Lefebvre turned his thoughts to this future and finished the consecration ceremony, Dom Gérard for his part, seated in the back at the top of the slope, distanced himself.

Those Who Dissent

The Prior of Le Barroux, who found these words staggering, told his driver, Laurent Meunier, "The show has lasted quite a while, this meeting, all this applause! We have nothing more to do here. We are going back."

Followed by Jean Madiran, in the magazine *Itinéraires*, the monk deplored the "break" with Rome made by the prelate and most of the family of Tradition: "It is detrimental to the very Tradition of the Church to be isolated outside the visible confines of the Church."

Archbishop Lefebvre corrected this imprecise notion; in *Fideliter*, no. 70, he wrote: "But we *represent* the visible Church!. We are not leaving it! We have fought against what is called 'the conciliar Church' because we want the Catholic Church; would we have to return to this 'conciliar Church' in order to make it Catholic, so to speak? That is totally an illusion! The subjects do not make the superiors, but rather the superiors are the ones who make the subjects! In this whole Roman Curia, among all the bishops of the world, who are progressives, I would have been completely drowned, I could not have done anything, nor protect the faithful and the seminarians."

Optimism and Firmness

Of course the practical wisdom of the prelate from Ecône did not rule out "resuming the talks after a while" (he is optimistic).

"But then," he said, "I do not want to be put into the position of inferiority as in the spring of 1988, when I had to accept doctrinal requirements that are by no means ours! I will set my conditions: 'Do you accept *Quanta cura* of Pius IX, *Libertas* of Leo XIII, *Pascendi* of Saint Pius X, *Humani generis* of Pius XII?'"

But the purpose would never be to arrive at a definitive rupture with the See of Peter.

As early as 1979 he explained why he wanted to maintain relations, a dialogue with the Holy See, although he acknowledged that it was often "a dialogue of the deaf." "What is to be done about the authorities now in place? Shut ourselves up in our resistance as though in an ivory tower? I did not take the side of breaking off the dialogue with Rome. We must try, if possible, to convert them."

CHAPTER XXX

Charity of a Pastor
and Tact of a Leader

"Charity is patient," Saint Paul says (I Cor. 13:4). This statement reechoed throughout the life of Archbishop Lefebvre. Let us attempt a brief retrospective of his practice of this virtue, which seemed to be the leading virtue of Marcel Lefebvre.

In Dakar, he instilled in his priests a pastoral approach that was charitable but not liberal: "True charity is missionary, understanding toward sinners; it strives to know the development that led them into error or sin, but does this so as to be able to draw them patiently away from sin, because it is not charity to help leave their minds in error and their souls in sin."

Breadth of Vision and Inventive Zeal

During a priestly retreat in 1952, Father Gravrand was on the hot seat. "*Monseigneur*, Father Gravrand is enrolling polygamous pagans on a list of 'friends of the Christians'; he even gives them an identity card with their name, and all under the rubric of 'Friends of the Christians.' Isn't this leaving these polygamous men in ignorance of the laws of marriage and in their sin?"

"Listen," the Vicar Apostolic replied, "that's not a bad idea. These polygamists are not prepared to receive Baptism, but they will agree to be catechized, and when the obstacle of their polygamy is removed, maybe during a serious illness when they will agree to keep only one wife, they can be baptized. And while waiting, they will belong 'sociologically' to Christendom; they will have their children baptized and catechized, and little by little the village will become Christian."

"Moreover this is what the first missionaries in India and Africa did in the seventeenth century, even Saint Francis Xavier: they baptized great numbers of newborns and catechumens who were prepared rapidly; that may seem highly imprudent to us, but it was a question of forming a 'sociological mass' that could stand up to paganism. Do you understand?

"Let us not box ourselves into a sterile routine! Our predecessors in their day went ahead; if we too go ahead, we are being faithful to them. May your zeal be inventive and ingenious!"

But charity is able to be strong, too, and even to make use of force!

Charity and Authority

In Gabon, one day in 1942, he learned that a Christian had relapsed into polygamy (he took back a second wife or even several). It was necessary to save the Christian woman and to correct the guilty party. He related the story:

"Immediately I gathered several sturdy men, and we went to the guilty man's hut to take away his legitimate wife by force; she argued and cried, pretending that she did not consent, but in reality she was quite in agreement with us; it was all play-acting: she threw herself into the water and seemed to be trying to commit suicide. They brought her out, to her great joy. And she was confined to a hut belonging to the mission. Then, if the renegade wanted to get his Christian wife back, he had to come and promise to dismiss his concubines (false wives)."

Later, in Senegal in 1954, *Monseigneur* learned that on the Island of Fadiouth some Muslim merchants had got some Christians into debt and that in payment for the debt they now demanded that such and such a boy be handed over to them; he would be their slave and would become Muslim! Immediately the Bishop reacted with the same active charity for souls: "I'm putting that island under interdict! No more Masses or Sacraments until you have driven those merchants away!"

And the draconian measure had its effect: the Muslim merchants disappeared.

A Gift of Very Gentle Authority

In dealing with his priests, *Monseigneur* Lefebvre showed much-appreciated tact.

"Father Carron," he said one day in 1957 to one of his missionaries while taking hold of his sleeve, "come see me; I have something to tell you."

"At your service, *Monseigneur!*"

"Here, I have a problem: at the seminary I have to change Father So-and-so, but the other priest I was thinking of does not want this position as professor, and so ..." He did not have to finish his sentence.

"I understand, *Monseigneur*, you're the boss. Command, and I will obey!"

And thus Father Carron was taken away from the House for charitable works where he was getting lost in the social demands and was ruining his priesthood. He went on to become a good professor, but the Bishop would ask him to use a textbook or, if he wanted to conduct classes more freely, simply to comment on Saint Thomas and the Magisterium of the Church.

His confreres appreciated this kind of governance with kid gloves. Father Bussard, his Vicar General, testified to it: "It's a gift that he has, a special talent for very gentle authority. He does not put on the airs of a commander, but he certainly does command! He is not a ponderous bishop, an authoritarian bishop, no; but rather a bishop full of authority. He has principles but also kindness. That man is like a paradox: he is gentle and merciful.... For example, with regard to two priests whom he had to have called back to France: well, he ended up accepting one of them again. He is stricter with a rubric than with a person!"

"He leads men the way he drives his car," said Brother Christian, "he does not drive off full speed; he takes the curves smoothly, accelerating at the right moment. I call it 'the iron hand in a velvet glove.'"

"Yes," Father André Buttet said, "when *Monseigneur* comes to the seminary in Sébikhotane, if he has a remark to make, he does it without speaking louder, with his soft little voice: "Don't you think it would be good to …?""

"He is even able to respect the opinion of someone who does not share his views," said Archbishop Sartre of Tananarive. "In a meeting of the bishops' conference, he calmly listens to one side and the other, never showing strong disagreement. Then he does not hesitate to make his proposals. He gives his directives, knowing how to rely on the authority of the Holy See to assert them."

Later, he taught his seminarians of the Society how he did it. "No one is obliged to make the truth disagreeable! You listen attentively to your interlocutor, then you accept the part of the truth contained in what he says, and then you state your reservations."

Conviviality and Attractiveness

With his fellow diners at the seminary refectory, *Monseigneur* Lefebvre had the talent of "holy teasing," the victims of which were Father Le Boulch, a gentle Benedictine, or even Father Schmidberger, Superior General, his successor!

He was able to put people at ease and was at ease with everyone. At the table in Ecône, Father Louis-Olivier Dubuis, an occasional professor at the seminary, remarked: "He is exactly the same with an Archduke and an industrialist, just as kindly accessible. I have seen it and was quite struck by it, and I highly admired him. He was the same, and it was not forced; it was very pastoral."

Monseigneur Lefebvre had no equal in proposing a toast that was spiritual and humorous at the same time at the end of an ordination banquet.

Everywhere, Marcel Lefebvre showed human warmth and a remarkable ability to make contact.

CHAPTER XXXI

Strength and Gentleness

There were meetings, however, when Marcel Lefebvre, a man of dialogue, "dug in his heels" for the sake of the good. With regard to the "strong-minded" he was "a man who reacts." One then was liable to hear rather sharp words from a man who held his opinion or his decision tenaciously. That was rare, because usually he was "very quiet and calm," capable of putting up with a progressive-minded general councilor for six years. But self-control is the best indication of the virtue of fortitude.

"When a Gentle Man Sets Out to Be Strong ..."

When confronted with wrong-headed individuals, he preferred to remain silent rather than to argue, especially when the interlocutor was superior to him in rank or by his knowledge.

One day, invited to a meal by a friend, he found at his table his former fellow student, Msgr. Georges Leclercq, dean of the Catholic University in Lille; the latter held virulent modernist views, as Michel Lefebvre, who was present at the scene, related:

"Well, my brother Marcel did not open his mouth. And once he left, he confided to me: 'It is horrible what can be said, truly it is frightening!' But he did not seek to debate; it was as though he was paralyzed."

He sensed too clearly the futility of all debate when a first principle is denied by the interlocutor. Furthermore, he found it inconceivable that a scholar or a prelate should contradict doctrine.

"Above all," Father Marziac considered, "he has a deep respect for those who hold authority, a great respect for persons; he takes care not to humiliate."

One day in 1974, when he had to transfer a seminary rector, he said, after carrying it out: "Previously, I did not sleep for several nights because of it. It was the sword of Damocles over my head, before I asked him to go away."

This excessive delicacy was of a particular sort, because it never affected him in public but only in his person-to-person relations. It was a certain difficulty in communicating when the words would indicate a disparagement of someone else. In Marcel Lefebvre there was a contrast and at the same time a balance between the most tenacious self-assurance and the most delicate attention to others; this alliance forged in him a human, attractive personality which inspired trust and friendship. Many Spiritans who did not follow his opinions, like Father Michael O'Carroll, testified to this: "Oh, I was attached to that man! And I still am!"

Some people could not manage to reconcile "the two faces" of Marcel Lefebvre: "Your kindness is harsh," Jean Guitton would say to him on the eve of the episcopal consecrations.

Others judged him: "He is a proud man!"

"No," Father Louis Carron replied, even though he clashed with the Archbishop. "Personally he is humble; the proud thing is his doctrine! It is a formula!"

A fine formula, dear Father Carron! Your bishop was not a liberal, and thus he was altogether charitable *in re et in modo*, substantively and in his way of saying things.

"There was no man meeker than Moses," Father Mehrle said, "and yet he was the one who, carried away by holy wrath, broke the Tablets of the Law! (Ex. 32:19). When a gentle man sets out to be strong, he can go very far."

This reflection of the good Dominican Father (a professor in Ecône) on the subject of Archbishop Lefebvre was quite correct. But Marcel Lefebvre's strength lay more profoundly in the lively enthusiasm of his twenties, in the torch that he received at Santa Chiara; its flame devoured him and he wanted to transmit it.

Orator Without Realizing It

In spiritual conferences that he gave to his seminarians, he acknowledged, he was "rather soporific," although what he said was much more profound than what dear Father Barrielle taught according to Saint John Berchmans or Saint Louis de Gonzaga.

But in public, the style of his conferences became livelier, full of images, sometimes mocking or even ironic. His rhetoric became biting when he got particularly eloquent or confronted the media crowd (journalists and reporters), whom he could both alienate by the political positions that he took and also win over by the fact that he was a resistance figure, disconcerting and intriguing at the same time. In Essen, Germany, speaking to six thousand persons, he denounced the liberal conciliar ecumenism.

"No longer enemies, but brothers! No more need to fight! Let's cease the hostilities! It is as though a worldwide medical congress decided: 'From now on, no more sickness: sickness is health! No more need for medical schools, hospitals. Make peace with sickness!'"

The applause of the amused listeners almost brought down the house. It was not surprising that the polls conducted by the media and the magazines declared Archbishop Lefebvre "rather sympathetic." The journalists themselves did not always do their job with him, so charmed that they sometimes forget to "skewer" him. For instance Henri Fesquet, a columnist for the newspaper *Le Monde*, who on the eve of the 1988 consecrations declared, "I'm going to make your boss crash and burn!" But he had to give up that plan.

A publicist from *Paris Match*, Robert Serrou, sketched in two lines the style of the preacher at the "Lille Mass" in 1976; he did not conceal his sympathy: "Although the tone is peaceful, the remarks are inflammatory, fiery darts. He is at the same time timid and bold, modest and full of assurance."

Usually he preached doctrine, doctrine alone, and he had some expressions that are brand new, like this unusual description of the Blessed Virgin: "She is neither a liberal nor a modernist nor an ecumenist; she is allergic to all errors and all the more so to heresy and apostasy."

He preached without any oratorical affectation. His preaching was not sentimental, it did not charm the heart; it nourished the intellect and moved the will. He was nevertheless sometimes an orator without intending it, when the Holy Ghost seemed to swoop down on him, seize him and inspire him. With the miter on his head during sermons for ordinations, he felt convinced that he can communicate; his voice became stronger and rose in pitch; he pointed with his finger and he set forth principles of combat and vengeful truths with regard to the enemies of the Church and those who corrupt the priesthood. Then the "timid man" became bold and the modest man full of assurance; in a person-to-person conversation, respect restrained him; in public he felt free and became a lion.

Father Boudelet recalled that he expressed the truths of the faith with remarkable precision. A lawyer like Yves Pivert even judged that Archbishop Lefebvre was an orator "in the sense that he convinces."

"This is a gift that he has: the gift of presenting evidence. It is like a fine speech for the defense. You cannot be of some other opinion. It is all in the way in which he conducts the argument."

"*Monseigneur*," a priest asked, "is a sermon a logical proof?"

"Of course, you must often pose problems, the problems of your people, and solve them. Simply cite Sacred Scripture, the lives of the saints. Conclude with some practical advice. But for the doctrine of the faith, do not prove it, affirm the faith! People try too much to prove it, to do apologetics. But the faith is not that; it is adhering to God who reveals His mystery. Your people already have the faith, in principle; they are therefore inclined to believe what the Church teaches. What they ask of you is to teach what God says, what the Church teaches. People try to prove too much. Affirm the faith!"

In his inspired moments, the Archbishop found inimitable affirmations, for example on the mystery of the Incarnation: "We have only one God, Our Lord Jesus Christ!"

"Our Lord is the only man who is God! Therefore He is King. Therefore He must reign, consequently he has something to say about everything."

What did he preach? The Incarnate Word, the God-man, Jesus Christ, His cross, His royalty, His priesthood: "This presence of God Incarnate in the history of humanity," he said, "can only be the center of this history, like the sun toward which everything travels and from which everything comes."

CHAPTER XXXII

The Founder and His Seminarians

With his seminarians, the founder was fatherhood itself, that "paternal authority" (as the statutes of his Society say), an authority which on the one hand is not authoritarian and which on the other hand does not demean itself in familiarity, and which is consequently beneficial: it does not crush the subject's personality but causes it to develop straightforwardly.

When leaving the refectory at 1:00 in the afternoon or at 8:00 in the evening, he liked to stay in the corridor, continuing a conversation with his professors or starting one with some seminarians. During the monthly community excursions, if it was winter, he could not resist the pleasure of personally starting a snow-ball fight. And once he was in his office, he received his young clerics at any hour, and they greatly enjoyed coming to try his patience by confiding this concern, or that obstacle to fraternal charity, this worry about a confrere who seemed "liberal" to them or on the contrary seemed to them to be very critical and self-centered. They were glad to calm their fears, to receive his counsels, to hear lessons from his experience.

"Be Formed to the Truth Before You Try to Combat Error!"

The seminarians were generally ardent, combative young men, but sometimes also a bit over-rational. One of them, Father Lancien, knocked at the founder's door.

"Come in! Sit down. How are you?"

"*Monseigneur*, in what spirit did you found the Society? Wasn't it to combat the conciliar errors, to thwart the liberal compromises, to conquer the Modernist dragon that is rising up again? Some confreres want no part of that combat. It seems to me, though, that we must be anti-liberal!"

"I understand the importance of the question; I will answer it in detail during the spiritual conference."

And that same evening, *Monseigneur* explained his thought with very special precision:

"The Society was not born in a spirit of disputation; it was born in the same way as all works created by God to remedy a deviation or lukewarmness in the Church. This is what I intended to do in giving you your statutes, which state the means of truly curing the failure of priests since before the Council: I proposed these means in our statutes: Thomistic teaching, common life, liturgical piety, missionary charity. This is what the founder of the Spiritans in the eighteenth century, Venerable Claude Poullart des Places, did: form holy, doctrinal priests." The following weeks, back from a short trip to southwestern France, during which he gave public conferences, he found at the door of his office young Father Beaumont.

"*Monseigneur*, of course we must not have a spirit of disputation; but you yourself give us the example of fighting for the faith, of the struggle against errors!"

"Understand me, now: I am a bishop; I must defend the Catholic faith, I must denounce errors. But you, dear Father, you have to be formed. I will explain this at the spiritual conference."

And that evening the founder returned to the fray, as they say. "Your first goal at the seminary is not to combat errors but to know the truth. You are here to be formed. Certainly, it is necessary for you to be up to date about modern errors so as to be able to restate the truth when you preach the Gospel someday. This is why I gave you that list of Catholic authors who fought against liberalism, Louis Veuillot, Cardinal Pie, Father Emmanuel Barbier, so that you might read them. But don't make the battle against error the chief aspect of your future apostolate. Some are obsessed by error to the point of forgetting to learn the truth and teach it; others, it is true, in contrast feel a repugnance against speaking about errors. Both the former and the latter are wrong. Let us not be above all 'anti-liberal' or 'anti-Communist.' You cannot dispel the darkness without having the light. You will obtain this light correctly only through prayer, sacrifice, mortification and holiness."

"Your Combat is Essentially Supernatural"

"But, *Monseigneur*, the Church is now submerged by unheard-of errors; we can't just let that happen. Holiness is in the first place the Catholic faith!"

"No doubt. But pay attention: We are not the first to combat these errors. Go to the school of the popes who have already denounced them. Therefore, study first and meditate on how the popes fought liberalism and Communism, for example how Pius IX in *Quanta Cura*, already a hundred years in advance, condemned the religious liberty of the Second Vatican Council! These popes were above all priests, spiritual men, penetrated by the desire to make Our Lord reign."

"Indeed," he continued, "your combat is a supernatural combat, against the powers of the devil and of the wicked angels. It is a combat of giants: giants of holiness, and not a combat of intellectual duels. By entering this seminary, you enter into the history of the Church, you enter into the combat much better than you could have done as students at the university. It is not on the natural level but on the level of divine grace."

"And the Constitution of the United States?"

"Thank you, *Monseigneur*," Father Littlejohn came to say, "but some of my American confreres have difficulty understanding that we must fight against freedom of worship, which to them seems to be ingrained in the customs of the United States."

"But what does the Constitution of your country say?"

"*Monseigneur*, it says nothing about it! Yes, it is the most extraordinary paradox. The name of God is not even mentioned in it, and the word 'religion' is positively banished from it. And yet, everybody is religious, belongs publicly to one 'church' or another and attends their Sunday services. Everywhere there are large numbers of churches of different Christian or non-Christian denominations, and back home there is no trace of what you sense in France: laicism and anti-clericalism. The atmosphere is imbued with religiosity. But to tell the truth, the Catholic religion was persecuted for a very long time, contrary to the equality of everyone before the law that is proclaimed."

"What a pile of contradictions! But the most serious one is the absolute separation of State and religion, and—except for the oath that Presidents take on the Bible (but what does that signify?)—the supreme authority of God, author of all things, persons as well as societies, is not invoked!"

"Our dollar bills all bear the inscription: 'In God we trust'!"

"Yes, I know, but is it faith, the theological virtue? Is it faith in a God One and Triune on which your republic is founded?"

"To tell the truth, *Monseigneur*, it is 'We the People,' in other words a mass of human beings 'born both free and independent' which freely decides to take this Constitution, for the sake of its peace and prosperity."

Taking Charles Maurras as his inspiration, Father Aulagnier objected: "This people is nevertheless made up of fathers and mothers of families and their children; therefore of heads of families and their members; of masters of a profession and their workers and apprentices; of lawyers and administrators; of founders and of those in the foundation. This 'people,' therefore, is not a mass of equal persons, but a flood of gratuitous services, a panorama of well-defined dependencies, a display of unilateral generous acts that the predecessor makes to the successor on the spiritual level, a set of pure hierarchies, the contrary of 'We the People'!"

Monseigneur, faithful to the spirit of dear Father Le Floch, objected in turn: "And what order, what peace can reign in a nation whose authority, thus artificially imagined to be at the base, doesn't depend on the Author of social human nature, God? And doesn't depend on the Prince of Peace, Our Lord Jesus Christ, Christ the King? How can we imagine for a single instant that a society can be indifferent to the existence of God, the source of all authority, and indifferent also to the presence of the Incarnate Word in the midst of the human race?"

"Certainly not, *Monseigneur*. But without meaning to reject God, or the cross of Christ, or of combating the Catholic religion, cannot society accept a *de facto* state of affairs and acknowledge that there is a place for all who think that they are honoring God as they are able? This is the question of my confreres."

"That is not the real question," the Archbishop replied. "What should concern you is a political order in conformity with human nature, and above all, the eternal salvation of your fellow citizens, through their entrance into the Catholic Church. Isn't that right? Leo XIII, in his Encyclical *Longinqua oceani*, recognized that in the United States ... I have the text right here, lines that are truly indulgent. I'll read them for you: 'For the Church amongst you, ... fettered by no hostile legislation, ... is free to live and act without hindrance. Yet, though all this is true, it would be very erroneous to draw the conclusion that in America is to be sought the type of the most desirable status of the Church, or that it would be universally lawful or expedient for State and Church to be, as in America, dissevered and divorced. The fact that Catholicity with you is in good condition, nay, is even enjoying a prosperous growth, is by all means to be attributed to the fecundity with which God has endowed His Church, in virtue of which unless men or circumstances interfere, she spontaneously expands and propagates herself; but she would bring forth more abundant fruits if, in addition to liberty, she enjoyed the favor of the laws and the patronage of the public authority.' This is a question of faith: either we believe in the divinity of Our Lord Jesus Christ or else we do not believe in it. And if we believe it, we are convinced that His social kingship best supports the possibility of the Church prospering and developing."

This is how we should understand the weakness, the crucial gap in this Constitution of the United States.

"Pass on a Truth That Does Not Belong to You!"

"Thank you, *Monseigneur*," Father Tissier said, "we needed these clarifications about the nature of our combat. But sometimes we have to discuss or argue with 'conciliar' friends, or even family members."

"Be careful! I remind you of a golden rule: I will not convince anyone by insulting my interlocutor or by despising him! But if I have true, selfless charity: *Caritas non quaerit quae sua sunt* [Charity seeketh not her own], Saint Paul says; if I do not want to prevail personally but rather to pass on a truth that does not belong to me, then I will convert others." "I would say, naturally," he concluded, "that the Society combats the liberal errors and deviations above all by its existence, by the firmness of its Catholic faith and by its missionary charity and that it is a solid stepping-stone and foundation stone for the restoration of the priesthood and the rebuilding of the Church."

A Fight That Inspires Enthusiasm

"What a job! What work you will have to accomplish, my dear friends! You are the 'little remnant' which nevertheless boldly carries the torch. Don't be afraid to show it. Don't be afraid to show that you are priests, traditional priests, the kind of priests that the Church has always intended to make, priests for the truth, priests for holiness!

"Ah! What a fine task, what a fine crusade you have ahead of you! The good Lord let you be born in an era of human history that inspires enthusiasm in young men like you. Just like the Machabees when they left the corrupt society in Israel at that time: they were only a few. Judas Machabeus found himself with 800 soldiers facing an army of 20,000. And he beat them."

"Well, then, be confident, dear friends! God is with you. He will not abandon you, any more than He abandoned us over the course of these twenty years!"

CHAPTER XXXIII

Archbishop Lefebvre Up Close

During the last twenty years of his life, whether in his dear seminary or on the road, his chauffeurs, the men who drove him by car, were the keenest observers and anecdotalists; they paint a close-up portrait of the Archbishop.

The Archbishop on a Road Trip

"There are seven or eight of us," Rémy Borgeat related, "often accompanied by our wife, and we take turns from one week to the next, receiving in advance from *Monseigneur* the itinerary for the trip. In the car, he follows the route on the map. He has an innate sense of direction and topography."

One day in Holland, accompanied by the young seminarian Jürgen Wegner who was driving, on the way to the house of the Spiritans in Gemert, he unexpectedly said: "Now, in one kilometer, you will turn right."

And he was not wrong: twelve years later, he still remembered exactly that fork in the road.

With him you could never lag. A discreet remark about the time let the driver understand—in that case Michel Porcellana, who nevertheless didn't dawdle—that he had to accelerate in order to arrive in time. The inevitable instances of speeding would be quickly forgiven by the indulgent policemen once the media had made him a popular figure. His purple skullcap carelessly placed on the back shelf of the vehicle would confirm the truth of what the driver would say: "Do you know whom you have stopped? It is Archbishop Lefebvre!"

"Oh! All right. All right. In that case, we will accompany you."

And there was the Archbishop going 160 kilometers per hour [95 m.p.h.] on a regular road, escorted before and after by two zealous, delighted policemen on motorcycles.

Then it was time for the news, and he would switch on the radio. After five or ten minutes, he would say: "Good, now let's begin the Rosary!"

After the Rosary, they would stop praying for a while. Then came a second Rosary and later on a third. In this way the whole Rosary would be recited.

During his days with the Spiritans, *Monseigneur* was content to buy two sandwiches and mineral water on the way for himself and his chauffeur. But now he was anxious to care for his friends who drove him. Marcel Pédroni tells the story:

"He knows respectable restaurants everywhere, even some that opened for him on days when they were closed. He recommends items on the menus to his drivers and never fails to go thank the chef, congratulating him on the guest book "for the fine *Champenoise* cuisine and the French-style service," which he appreciated. He willingly spends the night at a hotel, either so as not to disturb a priory at an unsuitable hour, or in order to take care of those who are accompanying him, and he does not go to sleep without having inspected his chauffeur's room and exchanging it, if necessary, for his. 'You are the driver; you need a quiet room. As for me, I'm deaf.'"

He thought of others first. One day, returning from Corrèze toward Clermont-Ferrand, he had one leg that hurt badly but refused to stop: "No," he said, "We must continue. The Reverend Father Bourdon is waiting for us in his new priory."

While making a tour for confirmations or to give conferences, he proved to be "charming, pleasantness personified," accessible to everyone, without taking offense at the thoughtlessness or the over-familiarity of the faithful toward him. It was not rare to hear "Hello, Bishop!" in the New World! He encouraged everyone and always found just the right thing to say, adapting to all sorts of situations: being more familiar with simpler folk, more delicate with the more refined, all things to all men.

One day he paid a visit to an elderly lady. Upon returning to the car, he explained to the priest who was driving him: "This is an old lady whom I just reconciled with the Church which she had abandoned after the condemnation of Action Française."

The Archbishop in His Office

Back in Ecône, Marcel Pedroni remarks, he would put his little suitcase and his briefcase down in his office and go immediately to the chapel if the Rosary was being recited there. "Community prayer has priority!" he explained to his chauffeur, although he had already prayed his entire Rosary along the way.

Then, after supper, he attacked the pile of mail that would be waiting for him; methodically, on his ever-uncluttered desk, he darkened with his fine, slanted, regularly aligned handwriting dozens of pages which he would then put into envelopes. Each of his correspondents would have a short, concise handwritten response to his concerns and a kind word at the conclusion.

In his office, on simple chipboard bookshelves, he had within reach a *Larousse* dictionary as a spelling reference, an *English Without Toil* [a popular conversational course] to brush up his English in preparation for trips to the United States, and an atlas with which to study the countries that he is going to visit. Higher up, with a Holy Bible, one would find the *Summa* of Saint Thomas, a French-Latin edition with commentaries taken from Cajetan, and still higher two collections of the pontifical acts of the popes, one chronological, the other thematic. With this light baggage of books, he was equipped to prepare his sermons and conferences and to nourish his spirit. Against another wall were new shelves for the collection of books that he had received as gifts, especially counter-revolutionary or anti-liberal literature; he gave the rest to the seminary library.

"Why bother with useless things?" he said. "In Africa, I received a large number of gifts: precious wood, animal skins, ivory. My friend Vito Roberti, who was nuncio in Africa, had established a museum of his rare objects. I am a religious. What good is it to keep all that? No one takes anything to heaven!"

And in his bedroom one found a hard, narrow bed, the same kind that his seminarians had, and bare walls with only a rudimentary crucifix and an ugly painting of the Assumption, to which were attached several photos of his deceased friends or priests. On a nightstand: his alarm clock and a plastic statuette of Our Lady of Lourdes with a bit of Lourdes water.

These were the mortified furnishings of a faithful religious.

CHAPTER XXXIV

Priest, Just a Priest

In some passive or "activist" priests one can see a discrepancy or separation between the interior life and exterior activity, between prayer and action. Witnesses did not observe that in Marcel Lefebvre. In his case, there was no opposition between prayer and the apostolate.

"Upon seeing him arrive in Dakar from Mortain, in all simplicity," one witness relates, "you might have said: This is a timid man who won't accomplish anything! Well, as a bishop he launched into action!"

Man of Prayer and of Apostolic Action

His Vicar General in Dakar described him: "He is at the same time a 'factory manager' and a spiritual man. That man does not have one moment of free time; he is perpetual motion. He says, 'From Madagascar or from Réunion, I follow my priests; I keep an eye on them!' And with all that, he is a very pious and very profoundly religious man."

The superior of his seminary in Sébikhotane saw him as "an example of that profound interior life, union with God, the source of spiritual fruitfulness."

On Sunday, in his cathedral in Dakar, kneeling on his prie-Dieu during Mass, Father Bussard related, "He seems totally absorbed in prayer."

And when he was at the altar, the seminarians in Ecône remarked later on, "His Mass is a model of modesty, precise gestures, recollection, without any stiffness or ostentation but characterized by dignified ease."

How Marcel Lefebvre Views His
Mass and His Priesthood

In Marcel Lefebvre we find only a harmony, a seemingly natural continuity between his Mass and his care for souls and for business. His whole life was unified and his Mass was what unified it. This had been true since his adolescence, when he served Mass and received Communion every day and soon launched into an apostolate to the poor.

Instinctively, and through his studies at Santa Chiara, he knew that the Mass is—as he liked to say—"the unbloody re-actualization of the Sacrifice of the cross." Oh, he did not look for a better definition, but sometimes he quoted the Council of Trent: "It is a visible sacrifice that represents the Sacrifice of the Cross, perpetuates the memory of it, and applies its saving grace to remit our daily sins."

Thus, knowing that the Mass is Calvary, perpetuated sacramentally, Marcel Lefebvre considered the Mass first as an atoning sacrifice, then the function and the dispositions of Jesus the Priest and that of His ministers, the priests.

Redemption and Atoning Sacrifice

"Oh! You know," he said to his seminarians, "open the *Summa* of Saint Thomas and you find first the presentation of the whole mystery of the Incarnation and of the Redemption."

"Yes, *Monseigneur*, our sins, Saint Thomas says, being acts of disobedience to God's law, are an offense against God, which has an almost infinite gravity because of the infinite majesty of God who is offended. In order to liberate mankind from the debt of their sins and from the debt of the punishments that they merit according to just divine vengeance, the Holy Doctor teaches, men would have to offer to God some reparation (or expiation or satisfaction) that pleased Him more than our sins displeased Him."

"And how can that be done, you wonder?"

"That was the good Lord's problem, if one may say so!"

"That's quite right, and God found that solution: only the incarnate Son of God, by suffering the Passion, could offer to God His Father in our place a condign satisfaction (one equal to the sin): on the one hand because of the immense love of charity and obedience by which He suffered; on the other hand because of the dignity of His life, which He gave as satisfaction and which was the life of a God-man, and finally because of the multitude and the severity of the sufferings that He accepted. This is why the Passion of Christ was not only sufficient but even a superabundant satisfaction for the sins of the human race, as Saint John says: 'And He is the propitiation (atonement, reparation) for our sins (which makes us pleasing to God): and not for ours only, but also for those of the whole world' (I Jn. 2:2)."

"*Monseigneur*, is it the case that God did everything for our salvation, to the point where nothing is left for us to do, as the Protestants think?"

"No, of course not. We must contribute our share of expiation, which has its value by virtue of the expiation of Jesus Christ, as Saint Paul says: 'in my flesh ... I fill up those things that are wanting of the sufferings of Christ, for His body, which is the Church' (Col. 1:24)."

"And how can we best offer our satisfactions to God?"

"The best and simplest way is by participating in the Holy Sacrifice of the Mass. Isn't that where Jesus presents again each day the offering that He made of His sufferings on Calvary? At the altar, through the priest, let us join the offering of ours to the offering that Jesus makes of His through the ministry of the priest."

The Priest's Role and Dispositions

"These are precisely the role and the dispositions of Jesus the High Priest and those of the human priest, His minister: you find this in the writings of dear Dom Marmion and in those of Father Garrigou-Lagrange; in a word, I would say:

"'Through His most holy Incarnation, the fact that God Himself takes charge of the soul of Jesus Christ confers on this Man unique attributes, rights and privileges: preacher, Savior, Priest and King. Consequently, all priesthood will only be a participation in the priesthood of Jesus Christ; all authority will be a participation in the kingship of Jesus Christ.'"

"*Monseigneur*, you even went so far as to dare to say in a sermon that we found striking: 'The human priest is established a priest through a participation in the grace of union, the grace that properly belongs to the human soul of the Incarnate Word. The priest is therefore by essence (by definition) and must be in act (in his actions) configured to Christ the Priest; *'sacerdos alter Christus'*: the priest is another Christ.'"

"Yes, dear friends, I had you read the exhortation *Haerent animo* by Saint Pius X to the Catholic clergy in 1908, in which our holy Patron draws the consequences of this doctrine:

"'Taking the place of Christ in the offering of the Sacrifice par excellence, which is perpetually renewed for the world's salvation, the priest must put himself in the same state of mind as the one in which Jesus Christ, the Spotless Victim, offered Himself to God on the altar of the cross.'"

But in his *Spiritual Journey*, composed in 1990 one year before his death as a spiritual testament that he left to his sons, Marcel Lefebvre best described the dispositions of Christ the Priest which must be those of the priest; he took as his inspiration Saint Paul to the Hebrews:

"Our Lord Jesus Christ, whose holy soul, assumed (taken up and possessed) by the Word, endowed from the beginning with the fullness of sanctifying grace and of charity, is inundated with the splendors of the beatific vision, is plunged into adoration of His Father and offers Himself in advance as a sacrifice, through loving obedience, to God His Father, so as to satisfy (expiate) the sins of mankind."

This was the fundamental attitude which Marcel Lefebvre, a priest, lived out in his prayer and in his priestly activity.

Devotion to the Sacrifice of the Mass

"*Monseigneur,*" Father Yves Le Roux asked, "what should be the characteristic devotion of the priest?"

"Devotion to his Mass! Certainly, since Saint Julienne of Cornillon in the Middle Ages, and recently too with Saint Peter Julian Eymard, the Church has developed devotion to the Real Presence of Jesus, and, specifically through Saint Pius X, devotion to Holy Communion. That is well and good.

"But," he added, "one might run the risk of forgetting the Mass itself! By considering the Eucharist only as the Real Presence of the God-man, or as the spiritual refreshment of the soul, one would forget that the consecrated Host is only the fruit of the Sacrifice! Thus, He whom we adore and receive is the Victim on Calvary. By attending—it is better for us to say, by participating in—the Mass and in receiving Communion, we participate in Our Lord's Victim status. If we forgot that, we would no longer be truly Catholic! To make ourselves victims with Jesus the Victim is the whole Christian spirit. Suffering and His offering are the most beautiful, the most profound, the most real thing in the Catholic religion!"

"Is this, *Monseigneur*, what the Society should live and preach?" asked the practical Father Coenraad Daniels.

"Exactly! But to this interior, spiritual aspect of the fruit of the Mass we must add the apostolic and social fruit: Since all the graces of Calvary are applied through the Mass, the Mass is essentially apostolic. The Society of Saint Pius X is apostolic because the Mass is apostolic."

"*Monseigneur,*" Father Kenneth Dean interrupted, "An indiscreet question, if I may: Is this what you meditate on in your prayer?"

"Yes, that is indeed what I meditate on: 'The more one studies the Sacrifice of the Mass, the more one perceives that it is truly an extraordinary mystery. It is truly the mystery of our faith. In it the priest appears as someone who does not belong to time, who almost passes into eternity, because all his words have the value of eternity. It is not a simple rite carried out today, it is an eternal reality that transcends time and has eternal consequences for the glory of God, in order to deliver the souls in purgatory and to sanctify our souls. Each Mass truly has the weight of eternity.'"

The Apostolic Fruit of the Mass

"Once again, *Monseigneur*," Father François Knittel then said, "how do you understand the Mass as being apostolic?"

"In each Mass the Precious Blood is shed sacramentally: for those for whose intention that sacramental immolation is celebrated: 'as a propitiation for the sins that we commit every day,' says the *Roman Catechism* of the Council of Trent; and also for the whole Church and for all human beings; but it is also necessary for them to have some contact with this Blood that was shed for them. They have this contact particularly by participating in the Holy Sacrifice. And I know this from experience; I related this in the sermon for my priestly jubilee in 1979; I still know it by heart."

"Tell us again, *Monseigneur!*" exclaimed Father Werner Bösiger.

"Oh, come on! There is nothing extraordinary about it. During that sermon, I even 'drew a blank,' had a moment when I lost the train of my thought. It had already happened to me before: a complete 'blank.' ... I mumbled a short 'Guardian Angel, help me!' and a fuse blew. And the whole Church was plunged into darkness. O Divine Providence! I had the time to find my place again, the light went back on and I continued my sermon as if nothing had happened! But here is a little of what I preached on my jubilee."

A Moral, Physical and Political Transformation!

"'Before, through my studies, I knew what the Mass was, this great Mystery of our Faith, but I had not yet understood all its value, all its depth, all its efficacy. I experienced it day by day, year by year, in Africa, and particularly in Gabon where I spent thirteen years of my missionary life. And there, I saw, yes I *saw* what the grace of the Holy Mass could do. I saw it in the saintly souls that some of our catechists were: these pagan souls, who had become Christian through Baptism, transformed by their attendance at Mass and their Holy Communions, these souls understood the mystery of the sacrifice of the cross, offered their sacrifices and their sufferings with Our Lord Jesus Christ and lived as Christians. I can give some names: Paul Ossima from Ndjolé, Eugène Ndong from Lambaréné, Marcel Mebale from Donguila, and I will continue with a name from Senegal, Mister Forster, the treasurer who made payments in Senegal, chosen for that very important office by his peers and even by the Muslims because of his honesty and integrity; these souls received Holy Communion fervently and became models and beacons to those around them; not to mention many other Christian men and women who were transformed by grace.

"'I was able to see these village of pagans who became Christians, being transformed not only spiritually, supernaturally, but also being transformed physically, socially, economically, politically, because these persons, despite the fact that they had been pagans, had become conscious of the need to perform their duty, despite the trials, despite the sacrifices, to keep their commitments and in particular their marriage commitments.'"

The Mass for the Social Reign of Jesus Christ

"Would you please, *Monseigneur*," asked the young, precise Father Patrick de la Rocque, "sum up, as though in a compendium, the fruit of the Mass for the social Kingship of Our Lord Jesus Christ?"

"The Mass is the proclamation of this Kingship: *Regnavit a ligno Deus.* God reigns through the wood of the cross, through the sacrifice of His Eternal Son. The Mass distributes the graces of the cross; it causes Christians to live in this spirit: in a spirit of sacrifice. Now, through sacrifice the order that was overturned by sin is reestablished: order in individuals, in families, in workplaces, in society. Father Dennis Fahey, one of my old classmates at Santa Chiara, puts it beautifully: 'The awareness of their unity with Christ at Mass, as co-offerers and co-victims, is what strengthened the Catholics of the early centuries with a view to the long battle for the complete recognition of the rights of God and of the Kingdom of Christ.'"

And from this example he inferred this splendid principle: "So that all human beings might participate in the Sacrifice offered by Jesus Christ as Priest, *God wills*, yes, *God wills* that society be organized under the government of Christ as King."

CHAPTER XXXV

Final Battles

"*Monseigneur*, not to be indiscreet, but what will you do in Paris?" asked Rémy Borgeat, one of the Archbishop's chauffeurs from Valais, on March 8, 1991, at the wheel of his powerful, steel-gray Mercedes.

"Rest assured that there's nothing secret about it, for once—Paris is not Rome."

The Temporal Involvement of Catholic Lay People

"Isn't it a quarrel with *Renaissance Catholique*, as someone told me?"

"Ah! So you know about it! It's a long story.... I followed sympathetically the university summer sessions of the Henri and André Charlier Center founded in 1980 by Bernard Antony with the support of Dom Gérard, Prior of Le Barroux...."

"Who are the Charliers?"

"Henri Charlier is a Catholic designer and sculptor whose art is at the same time traditional and strangely stylized: he gives to the saints whom he depicts an other-worldly formality, and their wide-eyed faces reflect their interior vision of God. The artist lived in Mesnil-Saint-Loup, the village in Champagne that was converted to a Christian liturgical life by Father Emmanuel, Dom Emmanuel André (1826-1903), curate of the village and Father Abbot of a monastery that he founded."

"Now it comes back to me! We passed by there one day."

"Yes, and I made frequent visits to Mesnil, where the Le Panse family, after the artist's death, has been maintaining his house with some of his works, and has kept up the spirit of Father Emmanuel, summed up in the 'little prayer' that they recite in Mesnil: 'Our Lady of Holy Hope, convert us.'"

"Yes, and the little statue of Our Lady of Hope is found in the church that was built by Father Emmanuel, isn't it? But who is André Charlier?"

"The brother of Henri Charlier. He was the former principal of the Des Roches School, which during the war withdrew to Maslacq in the Pyrenees. Dom Gérard, a former pupil of André Charlier, is heir to the thought of this master of Christian enthusiasm."

"Did Bernard Antony know the Charliers?"

"I don't think so, but he is a disciple of Dom Gérard. And with the support of the monk, Bernard Antony and his Charlier Center launched in 1983 a 'Pilgrimage of Christendom' from Paris to Chartres, which was at first meant to be 'a Traditional pilgrimage organized by laymen involved in temporal affairs, with the intention of forming a national Christian resistance and in a missionary spirit of reconciliation.'"

"It seems to me that the Society collaborated in these pilgrimages."

"Yes. The priests—many from the Society of Saint Pius X— who accompanied the pilgrims ceaselessly heard Confessions, absolved and accompanied the pilgrims while walking, and it was a moving spectacle to see so many Catholics, young and not-so-young, kneeling publicly in the mud or the dust of late Spring to receive the divine forgiveness for their sins."

"So far, *Monseigneur*, it's tip top [*i.e.* couldn't be better]!"

"Yes. But there was a rift between Father Aulagnier and Bernard Antony who, under his pseudonym Romain Marie, wrote a book entitled *Romain Marie sans concession* [*R.M. without concession*], which set forth the Reign of Christ the King imperfectly. Dom Gérard was clearer in his *Demain la Chrétienté* [*Tomorrow Christendom*]. But anyway, I thought that it would be more proper for such a pilgrimage to be directed by the clergy of the family of Tradition, especially by the priests of the Society of Saint Pius X."

"Romain Marie did not follow you at the time of the consecrations, right?"

"Like Dom Gérard, he thought that I was causing a schism, and dear Jean Madiran, who has been affiliated with that monk since Maslacq, followed them. This is why after the episcopal consecrations in 1988 the movement *Renaissance Catholique* was founded in France, with my approval, which took over from the Charlier Center in Society circles, for the pilgrimage and for Christian social action."

"But that is tip top!"

"Unfortunately, little by little, the directors of the new movements have tended to become emancipated, to make themselves independent of the structure of the Society and of its priories. 'We are not a pious association or a movement for religious instruction,' they say, 'but Catholic Action in the sense in which Saint Pius X understood it: to reestablish the reign of Christ the King in society. We are therefore relatively autonomous in relation to the clergy!'"

"Is that wrong?"

"The principle is correct," Archbishop Lefebvre replied, "but 'the high authority and the vigilance of the hierarchy,' as Saint Pius X demanded, must nevertheless be exercised by the clergy over this type of social and political action by lay Catholics, therefore by the clergy of the family of Tradition; otherwise there will be disorder."

"Does Paul Aulagnier view that as good order, in his District of France?"

"Father Aulagnier came to visit me in Ecône expressly to tell me: 'The difficulty is that our priests have no «ordinary» authority over the faithful, but only a supplied authority; therefore they cannot impose their authority as parish priests do.'"

"You already explained this, *Monseigneur*; the Society is an 'auxiliary clergy,' like in your French army there are auxiliary troops, often more skilled than the regular units!"

"That's quite right! You were acquainted with Father Bernard Waltz, who had been a non-assigned officer of a battalion of auxiliaries during the war in Indochina and told us stories about his feats in Fribourg...."

"Yes, *Monseigneur*, he told us in Ecône too about severity of the exploits that earned him his military medal!"

"He wears the ribbon on his cassock, and I found no fault with that! But to return to Paul Aulagnier, I proposed to him this guideline: 'The lay faithful, in their public activities, must become that much more docile to the superior guidance of the Society of Saint Pius X and of its clergy, since it is less able to demand obedience, exercising as it does only an auxiliary authority.'"

"And to make sure this rule is understood...."

"In order to prevent the difference of opinion with *Renaissance Catholique* from turning into a division between laymen and clerics, Father Aulagnier has just decided to found 'Circles of Tradition.'"

"What is their purpose?"

"Under the closer direction of the Society's priories and of the priestly societies and affiliated convents, they will provide doctrinal and spiritual formation for the lay faithful and will organize the annual pilgrimage fully dependent on the clergy."

"Good, then it's in order, *Monseigneur*!"

"It is not yet the ideal, far from it, since the Circles do not have as their main, specific purpose the subjection of the temporal order—the things of this world, let us say politics—to Christ the King."

"Well, then, *Monseigneur*, are you going to kick off the Circles?"

"Yes, in February, I agreed to come and preside at the founding meeting of the Circles of Tradition. There I want to recall the dependence of Catholic laymen with respect to the clergy. But you know that I have not felt very well for some time now, and so I entrusted this trip to you, a neighbor of Ecône and one of my experienced chauffeurs...."

The Trial of Illness and Death

Monseigneur Lefebvre would never arrive in Paris. In Bourg-en-Bresse, where he spent the night, he woke his chauffeur at three o'clock in the morning. "This won't work. Let's go back to Ecône!"

Just before reaching Martigny, a city located 12 kilometers [7.4 miles] from Ecône, he asked: "Let's go to the hospital. *Monsieur* Grenon will have me admitted there. But before that, I have something to take to Ecône."

In the corridor of the cloister: "Ah! You are bringing *Monseigneur* back to us already!" the seminary rector exclaimed.

"Yes, but nearly dead," Rémy Borgeat replied quickly. "I'm taking him to the hospital in Martigny."

Father Denis Puga accompanied the sick man in the car: "We are all praying for you, *Monseigneur!*"

God demanded of His servant one last battle: sickness and accepting death.

For some time he had been suffering from digestive complaints. He did not sleep, his heart "keeps stopping and starting." The scanner in Martigny revealed an intestinal tumor. They operated on him, and a tumor "the size of two grapefruits" was removed. He felt better and joked with the nurses.

"You're getting a good deal with me. I'm paying the full rate but you're not feeding me!"

His priests came to see him. He had received Extreme Unction. He was at peace.

"If I die, it's just as well. Better to do it now while I still have all my wits. Later, with my faculties diminished and no longer knowing what I might say, some would claim: 'He changed his mind, he repented.'"

On March 24, he had suffered a pulmonary embolism; it was painful for him to take a breath. Ecône was alerted at 11:30 p.m. The seminarians got up and prayed. The Rector, Father Michel Simoulin, was at the dying man's bedside. On March 25, at 3:25 a.m., the suffering Archbishop left his body forever and his face regained its serenity. Father Schmidberger, Superior General, having arrived from Rickenbach, closed the eyes of his beloved father.

It was Monday of Holy Week, but also the Feast of the Annunciation, the day when joy was announced to the world and when a new Life awakened in the Virgin's womb.

On Easter Tuesday, April 2, 1991, a crowd dressed in mourning colors filled the meadow of the seminary in order to participate in the founder's funeral Mass, to hear the funeral oration given by Father Schmidberger, and to see the absolution given successively by the deceased man's four sons in the episcopate. Then the casket with the mortal remains, carried by his priests on their shoulders, slowly went back up toward the vault of Ecône. The overcast sky brightens suddenly and joyous sunlight illumined the Alps and the valley. Twenty thousand souls sensed deep down that this was life that was passing and continuing. On the book of condolences, a "high-ranking Catholic" who lived this life of the Church's Tradition thanks to *Monseigneur* Lefebvre, wrote these rapid lines:

"Thank you for intervening, for saving the priesthood and for being our standard and for offering yourself as a holocaust to save your people."

Several weeks later Cardinal Silvio Oddi, more or less a friend, stopped by the vault in Ecône. He put his hand on the Archbishop's tombstone, on which were engraved these words by the Apostle: *"Tradidi quod et accepi"*: "I handed on what I also received," the phrase that he wanted to have engraved on his tomb.

The Cardinal then said aloud: "Thank you, *Monseigneur!*"

And he added: "He loved the Church too much!"

No! Not "too much"! Charity has no limit; it would be impossible to love Our Lord or His priesthood or His Church too much. Our Lord Jesus Christ loved us to the end: *"in finem dilexit"* (Jn. 13:1). *"Propter nimiam caritatem suam qua dilexit nos Deus"* (Eph. 2:4): because of the exceeding charity with which He loved us, God sent His Son to earth.

In Rome, at the age of eighteen, didn't Marcel Lefebvre, with all his heart as a future priest, for the love of God, of souls and of the Church, give himself, commit himself to a crusade for Christ the Priest and King? "And this crusade," he said, "can require martyrdom."